Think Like a Teacher,

Act Like a Parent

By James C. Harden, PhD

Copyright © 2013-2014 by James C. Harden, PHD.

All rights reserved. No part of this publication may be reproduced, distributed, or transmitted in any form or by any means, including photocopying, recording, or other electronic or mechanical methods without the prior written permission of the publisher, except in the case of brief quotations embodied in critical reviews and certain other noncommercial uses permitted by copyright law.

"James"

Success does not happen without support. Over time, I have had many supporters and "life investors." Though I cannot name and thank them all, I would certainly be remiss if I failed to acknowledge my greatest supporter. This movement would probably not have happened without the constant encouragement of my father and namesake, James Carter Harden Jr.

In life, not everyone has the opportunity to meet his or her hero. I was blessed to be raised by mine!

(My wife, Lashonna; my mother, Mary; and my siblings were great contributors as well. My dad is just a bit more vain and would love to see his name in print.)

Dedication

Throughout my life I have had the great fortune of learning from several mentors. Each of them watered this "educational seed" that God planted deep within me. Over time, this seed sprouted into a plant, which now bares fruit. This book is but a small portion of fruit which I am honored to share with you.

Rather than naming and thanking each of them, I believe this dedication is best spent sharing some of their wisdom and advice.

"Ride the road of education to its natural ending."

"With Jesus and education, you are unstoppable!"

"If you think education is expensive; what do you think ignorance costs?"

"People suffer from the lack of education."

"If you educate a man; you educate but one. If you educate a woman; you educate the generations."

"If a son is uneducated, let his father perish!"

"Education is our society's greatest equalizer."

"Education is the most powerful weapon you can use to change the world."

Table of Contents

A Couple Notes from the Author **1**
Purpose: 1
How to read this book..1

Introduction **3**
Education Pays! 3
The Student, the School and the Family 4
Circle of Blame 5
The Stool Analogy 6
Multiple Intelligences 6
Parent-Teacher Conferences 7

Chapter 1: Think Like a Teacher **9**
Question 1 12
Depth of Knowledge 16
Question 2 17
Documentation Log 19
Question 3 21
Question 4 26
Question 5 29
Question 6 32
Learning Style Inventory (SAMPLE) 34
Characteristics of Learning Styles...........................38
Question 7 44
Question 8 47
Maslow's Hierarchy of Needs................................49
Question 9 51
Question 10..54
Question 11..56
Individualized Student Success Plan 59
My Goal for This Week 62

Chapter 2: Act Like a Parent.....................................**63**

Question 12.. 64

Ten Words your Student Must Know to Perform Well on
Tests! 66

Question 13.. 67

Question 14.. 69

Question 15.. 71

Question 16.. 74

Question 17.. 78

Question 18.. 80

Question 19.. 82

Question 20.. 86

Chapter 3: School Discipline............................**89**

Discipline Overview 89

Frequently Asked Questions: 91

Chapter 4: Special Education (In Plain English) ...**101**

IEP vs. 5-0-4 Plan 103

Sample IEP 111

Chapter 5: A Short Conclusion...........................**127**

About the Author...**129**

A Couple Notes from the Author

Purpose:

Many feel our schools are failing. The purpose of this book is not to support or deny any such claims but to empower parents with a few tools to ensure their students receive the best educational experience possible. Knowing who to talk to and what questions to ask will provide you with insight needed to navigate the complex webs of public and private education systems.

Education is said to be society's greatest equalizer. Increased education can provide for increased salaries, social status, and opportunities for your family for several generations.

How to read this book.

This book should be considered a manual that can be followed, but not an outright piece of doctrine which must be followed to the letter. The essence of this book is not meant to judge teachers, schools, or parents. We focus instead on doing what is best for your child. (Which is what everyone want regardless of our varying definitions of success.) The greatest gift we can give our children is a high-quality education!

This book is broken into four major sections: Think Like a Teacher, Act Like a Parent, School Discipline, and Special Education Laws. Each section is filled with questions, answers, and commentary. This book is not an exhaustive list of educational issues. Further, I cannot provide a guarantee your child will make the honor roll or be

Think Like a Teacher, Act Like a Parent

accepted to Harvard because you purchased this book. However, I can guarantee if you read this book **and** follow the recommendations, your child will receive the priceless gift of an improved education.

Introduction

Education Pays!

A wise person once said, "Money is not everything, but it certainly has a way of easing your nerves!" For most of us, increased education leads to increased salary. Below is a simple chart showing how earning potential relates to education level.

Unemployment Rate 2011 (Percent)	Education Attained	Median Weekly Earnings 2011 (Dollars)
2.5%	Doctoral degree	$1,551
2.4	Professional degree (i.e. J.D. or M.B.A.)	$1,665
3.6	Master's degree	$1,263
4.9	Bachelor's degree	$1,053
6.8	Associate degree	$768
8.7	Some college, no degree	$719
9.4	High-school diploma	$638
14.1	Less than a high school diploma	$451
7.6	All Workers	$797

Think Like a Teacher, Act Like a Parent

Over the course of a 30-year career, the college graduate will earn close to $1 million more than a person with only a high school diploma. Further, it is estimated by 2016, more than 65% of all jobs will require training, a degree, or certification beyond a high school diploma. Which side of the graph would you like to represent your child?

Source: Bureau of Labor Statistics, Current Population Survey.
Note: Data are for persons age 25 and over. Earnings are for full-time wage and salary workers.

The Student, the School and the Family

We are given many gifts throughout our lives. Imagine taking your most precious gift to a complete stranger's house, leaving it there for eight hours, and expecting that gift to return in better condition than when you left it. If you are anything like me, you would be very afraid to drop anything valuable off with a complete stranger. You would probably do all the research possible to ensure this complete stranger is trustworthy and capable of caring for your gift. Following the extensive background check, if you choose to drop off this valuable gift, you will probably call hourly and to check on its well-being.

I am amazed at how many people drop their children off at school and expect complete strangers to return their children in better shape than when they left.

Think of your car. If you dropped your car off at the mechanic, how long would you wait before you called to check on it? What if you do not understand what the mechanic is saying? What if you are not satisfied with the work? If the mechanic messed up or failed to improve the car's performance, would you consider hiring an attorney to assist in straightening out the mess?

Introduction

Now instead of a mechanic and your car, consider school and your children. Do you pay closer attention to the handling of your car than to the handling of your children? Think about it!

Quick Quiz: (Please take this one question quiz.)

What will you do if your child is struggling in school?
  A. Blame your child and make him/her study harder.
  B. Get angry with the school. Call the teacher and give him a piece of your mind!
  C. Sit back and wait for things get better.
  D. Work with the school to create a success plan for your child.

My prayer is that you chose D, and maybe a little bit of A. What actions should you take? I'm glad you asked! Keep reading!

Circle of Blame

Many people believe our education system is flawed. As vehement as people are to point out the errors, it seems like no one wants to take responsibility for the solution. Rather than collectively owning the problem, many fingers are being pointed in every direction. This has become one great "circle of blame."

Teachers: "Parents need to be more involved with their child's education!"

Parents: "Teachers today do not care about students!"
Government: "We are falling behind the rest of the world."
Conservatives: "We need voucher programs and more competition."

Think Like a Teacher, Act Like a Parent

Liberals: "Our schools and teachers need more money."

Everyone: "When I was a kid, I walked three miles to school, uphill both ways!"

Blah, blah, blah! WHO CARES!? Hello, people! What about the kids? What do they want? What do they deserve? What are you going to do about it? This book attempts to intervene, interfere, and break the circle of blame.

The Stool Analogy

If properly supported, every student has the ability to succeed. Think of a stool with three legs. If one leg is taken away, the stool cannot stand. Now place a student on the seat of this stool. The stool represents student success. The legs represent the student, the school, and the family. If all three of these legs are aligned, the stool will stand and the student will achieve. With just one leg missing, the stool and the student will tumble.

Multiple Intelligences

Rest assured... your child is brilliant. Albert Einstein once said, "Everybody is a genius. But if you judge a fish by its ability to climb a tree, it will live its whole life believing that it is stupid or inadequate."

Everyone is smart in his or her own way. Again, schools have the responsibility of assisting you in maximizing your child's potential. From my experience, schools are able and parents are willing. We just have to figure out how to get these two entities on the same page.

Introduction

Parent-Teacher Conferences

Have you ever been invited to your child's school to discuss grades, behavior, progress, etc.? Then, when you arrive, you are bombarded with tons of erroneous pedagogical rhetoric (school/teacher babble that no one understands)? This almost seems like the conference is designed to make you feel like an inadequate parent. As a parent, you are left thinking, "Was the purpose of this conference, to intimidate me?"

(Note for educators: If you are reading this book, be honest. Do you really think parents know and care what RtI, PLCs, FBAs, IEPs, SLTs, 504s, Dibels and NAEP scores are? Heck, as a veteran educator, I am not sure if I remember what all of that stuff is!)

Parent-Teacher Conferences

Have you ever been invited to your child's school conferences, grades, behavior, progress, etc.? Then, when you arrive, you are bombarded with tons of enormous pedagogical jargon (school/teacher babble that no one understands)? This almost seems like the conference is designed to make you feel like an inadequate parent. As a parent, you are left thinking, "Was the purpose of this conference to humiliate me...

Chapter 1:
Think Like a Teacher

In approximately twenty years of service in public schools, I have yet to come across parents who do not love their children. In speaking with and counseling hundreds of parents, concerning their child's education, I have just about heard it all. But never once have I heard a parent say that they do not want a "good education" for their child, or that they do not want their child to participate in college or some kind of post-high school education. Furthermore, I have come to realize most parents are doing their best to prepare their children for successful school experiences.

In fact, I have witnessed many parents bend rules to send their child to a "good school." As an educator working in various educational settings, I have learned to question the concept of a good school. I am not saying all schools are equal in academic performance. Nor do I question the parent's intention to get their child in the highest performing school. However, I have learned that great and poor quality education happens in every school.

Sending a student to school can seem like something of a crapshoot. As a parent, your job is to control the odds as much as possible. I understand wanting to send your child to a good school, but instead of focusing on a good school, your focus should be on ensuring a good education.

A good school versus a good education lies largely in the hands of the parent. So I ask you: What are you doing to

Think Like a Teacher, Act Like a Parent

ensure your child gets a good education? Even if you can't get your child into a "good school," you have the responsibility of providing them with a good education. Remember, you are responsible for your child. A good education starts at home and begins prior to the student stepping one foot in any school. A good education happens between three o'clock and eight o'clock in the afternoon/evening (when your child is at home with you). A good education happens on weekends and in the summertime or any other break from school. Good schools are great. A good education is better!

In some instances, there is a major disconnect between what teachers expect and what parents teach at home. Many times, student success is determined by the student's ability to adapt to what's being taught at school as opposed to what is being taught in the home. *Chapter 1: Think Like a Teacher* will provide you with an essential understanding of the school/teacher/student interaction. With this bit of knowledge, you can better advocate for your child and use the power of education to increase their life opportunities.

In a nutshell, there are four major points in this chapter that you need to take in and think about:

1. Schools are generally good places and offer educational opportunities for all children.

2. Providing a good education is the teacher's job, but a parent's responsibility. (What happens in your house is far more important than what happens in the White House or the schoolhouse.)

Chapter 1: Think Like a Teacher

3. A good education trumps a "good school."

4. Teachers are mostly hard-working professionals who love children and deserve much honor and respect!

Think Like a Teacher, Act Like a Parent

Teacher/School Centered Question

Question 1

What is your teaching style, and what strategies do you use to engage students?

Purpose of the question:
Not every student learns the same way. Factors like culture and age, among others, can heavily determine a child's learning style. For example, Michelle grew up in a very traditional Native American household where her parents told her many stories. It's likely her learning style may be auditory. On the other hand, Steve's dad is a mechanic. Steve spends lots of time in the shop learning from his father, so his learning style may be kinesthetic (hands-on).

There is no right or wrong method of learning, but there are several different ways of learning. For this reason, teachers must use varied approaches when presenting lessons. **Teaching is facilitating learning, not lecturing.** Teachers must do whatever it takes to make every child successful, especially yours!

The concept of using various methods is referred to as *differentiated instruction.*

Expected answer:
> "I differentiate instruction to meet the needs of all learners."

> If you receive this answer, be sure to ask the teacher, "How?" and, "How do you know when the students understand?"

12

Chapter 1: Think Like a Teacher

Unacceptable answers:

"There are too many students in my class, so I just teach straight down the middle."

"We do a lot of memorization of facts in my class."

What to do if the teacher gives an unacceptable answer:
Memorization is not really learning. We want our children to think and make life decisions based on their personal interpretations of facts. We want our children to think for themselves and become leaders. If a teacher says they only teach one way, politely suggest to them your child's style of learning calls for the teacher to teach more than just one way. Also, schedule an appointment to meet with the principal (immediately) to share your concern. The principal may say students cannot change teachers. In all reality, changing student schedules may be difficult, but it is not impossible! Remember, we are talking about your child. Research suggests one bad teacher can damage a student for life. The principal and/or teacher may not like you, but that relationship is temporary. The relationship with your child is forever. Furthermore, the principal is likely aware of a poor teacher, and you are probably not the first to voice concerns.

Remember... if you have a concern with a teacher, do not wait. Make the principal aware immediately. Early reporting will reduce the damage of poor teaching.

Think Like a Teacher, Act Like a Parent

Depth of Knowledge (DOK) assists in understanding the learning process from instruction, to the student's interaction with the presented content. Teachers are taught to frequently ask students questions, listen to the answers, and judge the students level of understanding. If the teacher believes that the student has successfully received the information, then the teacher is free to move on with the next lesson. However, if the teacher believes that the students did not receive and understand the information, then the teacher should seek alternative methods of presenting the same information. This concept is referred to as *"Differentiated Instruction,"* which we have mentioned already.

According to the concept of DOK, there are four levels of activities that teachers can engage their students with. Level 1 is the lowest level of teaching and will produce the lowest levels of learning. However words and exercises associated with Level 4 ensure the highest level of teaching and learning is happening within the classroom. Below is a table explaining each level.

Chapter 1: Think Like a Teacher

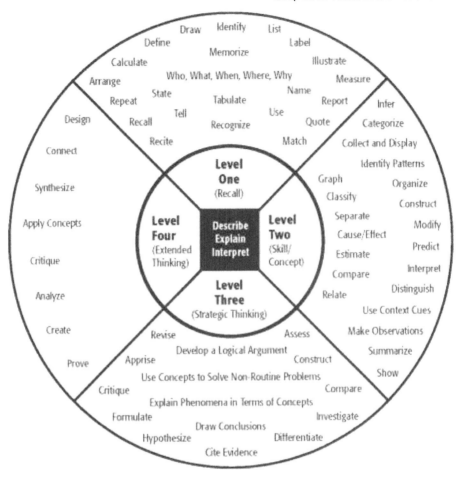

Think Like a Teacher, Act Like a Parent

Depth of Knowledge

Level One Activities	Level Two Activities	Level Three Activities	Level Four Activities
Recall elements and details of story structure, such as sequence of events, character, plot and setting. Conduct basic mathematical calculations. Label locations on a map. Represent in words or diagrams a scientific concept or relationship. Perform routine procedures like measuring length or using punctuation marks correctly. Describe the features of a place or people	Identify and summarize the major events in a narrative. Use context cues to identify the meaning of unfamiliar words. Solve routine multiple-step problems. Describe the cause/effect of a particular event. Identify patterns in events or behavior. Formulate a routine problem given data and conditions. Organize, represent and interpret data.	Support ideas with details and examples. Use voice appropriate to the purpose and audience. Identify research questions and design investigations for a scientific problem. Develop a scientific model for a complex situation. Determine the author's purpose and describe how it affects the interpretation of a reading selection. Apply a concept in other contexts	Conduct a project that requires specifying a problem, designing and conducting an experiment, analyzing its data, and reporting results / solutions. Apply mathematical model to illuminate a problem or situation. Analyze and synthesize information from multiple sources. Describe and illustrate how common themes are found across texts from different cultures. Design a mathematical model to inform and solve a practical or abstract situation.

Chapter 1: Think Like a Teacher

Question 2

What is your preferred method of communication? How often should I expect to hear from you?

Purpose of the question:

Much like any other relationship, communication is the key to success. You must be in constant communication with your child's teacher. The teacher and other school personnel should know your name without you having to introduce yourself soon after the school year begins.

Asking questions about communication will allow you to set the tone for the relationship. In a nutshell, it lets the teacher know that you expect to hear from him/her regularly and are open to various forms of communication. These communications from teachers do not have to be long-winded, and may include:

    A. Weekly phone calls
    B. Email detailing the upcoming week
    C. Weekly newsletter
    D. A "check-n-connect folder"

It is important for you and the teacher agree upon the method of communication to best support your child.

17

Think Like a Teacher, Act Like a Parent

Expected Answers:

"I send weekly reminders/newsletters home every Friday."

"I can always be reached by email. I try to return every message within 24 hours."

"Our school uses an automated call system to remind parents of upcoming events."

"I do all I can to reach every parent. What form of communication do you prefer?"

Unacceptable Answers:

"I only contact parents when there is a concern."

"I have 25 students in class, so it is tough to communicate with everyone."

"I only communicate by email."

What to do if the teacher gives an unacceptable answer:

- Contact the principal

- Document every attempt to contact the teacher

- Keep calling

- Show-up at school five minutes before dismissal and request an after school meeting with the teacher

*Please keep in mind teachers are humans too. They have their own lives and families away from the school, so be considerate of their time. Being as "to the point" as possible saves everyone time and addresses the real issues at hand.

Chapter 1: Think Like a Teacher

Documentation Log

Student's Name_____

School Year _____

Date/ Time	School Personnel	Purpose	Mode	Notes/Outcome
			☐ Conference ☐ Email ☐ Note/Letter ☐ Telephone	
			☐ Conference ☐ Email ☐ Note/Letter ☐ Telephone	
			☐ Conference ☐ Email ☐ Note/Letter ☐ Telephone	
			☐ Conference ☐ Email ☐ Note/Letter ☐ Telephone	
			☐ Conference ☐ Email ☐ Note/Letter ☐ Telephone	
			☐ Conference ☐ Email ☐ Note/Letter ☐ Telephone	
			☐ Conference ☐ Email ☐ Note/Letter ☐ Telephone	
			☐ Conference ☐ Email ☐ Note/Letter ☐ Telephone	
			☐ Conference ☐ Email ☐ Note/Letter ☐ Telephone	

Think Like a Teacher, Act Like a Parent

"If it is not written, it is not real." It is essential for the parent to keep good records of all communication with school personnel. Teachers and principals speak with hundreds of people and answer hundreds of questions on a daily basis. A simple Documentation Log like the one above will assist in making sure all parties are held accountable for all educational decisions and agreements. Should there be any disputes, principals, superintendents, school boards, and even judges consistently ask for documentation of conversations. So it's best to be prepared for such a worst case scenario.

Chapter 1: Think Like a Teacher

Question 3

What is your preferred method for teaching reading? How will you keep my child interested in reading?

Purpose of the question:
Reading may be the single most important skill taught in schools. More than simply reading, it's important your child learns to locate and identify key information within a text. There are five necessary components for a student to be a good reader:

1. Phonemic Awareness — knowing the sounds each letter makes

2. Phonics — knowing how each letter looks and sounds

3. Fluency — ability to read with expression and at the right speed without stumbling on a word

4. Vocabulary — ability to define words and know when to use them

5. Comprehension — understanding what was read

There are two main philosophies for teaching reading:

1. Whole word instruction — seeing a picture and a word together and memorizing the words and pictures together

2. Phonics — learning to read by pronouncing the sounds made by each letter

Think Like a Teacher, Act Like a Parent

I believe the best readers learn by way of phonics. Phonics creates a sense of independence as the child attempts to pronounce new words without any help. Though your child's teacher may not be a reading specialist, they must have an understanding of how to teach this vital skill. More importantly, YOU have the responsibility of teaching your child how to read and practice reading on a daily basis even before they begin school.

Don't know where to start? Here are a few pointers:

1. Go to your local thrift shop and garage sales to purchase books.

2. Make frequent visits to the library.

3. Let your child see you read books.

4. Ask your child what he or she is interested in reading about.

Expected answers:

"I teach using phonics."

"We have special support programs to assist our emergent readers. These programs are temporary, and the students are only in the program as long as necessary. We assess them every week to determine their progress and set goals to help move them out of the support program."

"Before going on our weekly library trip, I ask the student what books or topics may interest them."

"I ask parents to add to our class library by donating books."

Chapter 1: Think Like a Teacher

"I encourage students to read magazines, write songs and stories, and other such tasks to increase their love for literacy."

Unacceptable answers:

"I just use the textbook to teach reading."

"Children need to learn to read to appreciate the classics."

"I'm not a reading teacher."

What to do if the teacher gives an unacceptable answer:
- Expose our child to many styles and genres of books.

- Listen to audiobooks in the car.

- Regularly discuss books with your children.

- Let your child witness you reading.

- Create some type of reading reward program at home.

* Before pointing a finger at the school, do an internal assessment. Are you making sure your child practices reading at home? Do you read with him/her? It's never too late. Make your child turn off the tablet, computer, cellphone, video game, television, and have them pick up a book instead!

Think Like a Teacher, Act Like a Parent

Why is reading so important?

To fully understand the benefits of reading aloud to children, we need to look at the big picture. Reading 20 minutes a day will add up significantly during the years leading up to kindergarten. Children typically enter kindergarten at the age of five, so we need to look at the power of reading 20 minutes a day from the ages of birth to five years.

20 minutes x 30 days = 600 minutes or 10 hours per month

10 hours x 12 months = 120 hours per year

120 hours x 5 years = 600 hours over 5 years

A typical public school system is in session for 180 days each school year. Each day is made up of approximately five hours of total instruction time. A school day is certainly longer, but what is important is the total instruction time. Easily 40% of all instruction time during the school day is given to administrative matters, behavioral issues, and other non-instructional events. This leaves only three hours of total instruction time in a typical school day.

3 hours x 180 days = 540 total hours per school year

Now think back to when you were in school. How many times did you fall asleep in class? How often did you daydream or not pay attention in general? How many days were you at school when you didn't really feel well? For the typical student, this may be a lot! Realistically, there might be 540 hours of total instruction time per school year, but the "true" learning time is significantly less.

24

Chapter 1: Think Like a Teacher

Let's contrast this situation with the power of reading 20 minutes a day to our young children. If you read to your child for 20 minutes a day throughout all the years leading up to kindergarten, you will have provided 600 hours of instruction time to your child. Looking at straight numbers, 600 hours through 20 minutes a day is more total hours than a typical school year, which has approximately 540 hours of instruction.

The true "power" and benefits of reading aloud to children really come into play when we look at the total amount of learning time. It is easy to see that 100% of the 600 hours accumulated from reading 20 minutes a day is "true" learning time, typically enjoyed by a child who is interested, engaged, and in a loving environment conducive to learning. Contrast that to the school setting. How often are our children really interested and engaged? It definitely isn't 100% of the time. As you can tell, just 20 minutes a day can significantly improve your child's education.

Think Like a Teacher, Act Like a Parent

Question 4

What is your classroom management philosophy? How do you enforce it?

Purpose of the question:

A veteran educator once told me a bad teacher spends about 50% of class time teaching and about 50% of their time trying to manage the classroom. However, a good teacher spends 95% of their time teaching and only 5% of their time managing the class. From someone else, I might have taken this information with a grain of salt; however, this educator was twice the statewide Teacher of the Year.

The ability to manage a classroom is often the difference between a successful teacher and a failing teacher. When asking about the teacher's philosophy on classroom management, there are a few things to listen for:

- Relationships
- Organization
- Communication
- Creativity

It is very difficult to modify the behavior of a stranger. It is also difficult to sincerely correct the misbehavior of an enemy. Discipline is based in relationships, not force!

Think back to when you were a child: would you rather get a spanking or make your mother cry? Spankings come and go. Mother's tears come from a broken heart, disappointment, and failed expectations. (I would rather the spanking.)

Chapter 1: Think Like a Teacher

Remember substitute teachers? Oh, happy day! A stranger was taking over the class for a day, and we did not have to listen because we would probably never see this adult again.

An old cliché' reminds us; "Idle time is the devil's workshop." This is very true of students. An unorganized teacher or a teacher who gives students free time is unacceptable! In college, teachers all learn the best way to manage a classroom is to have a good lesson plan. But let's be honest, some of us have children we cannot manage. Every day we hope the child does not embarrass the family's good name. In this case, it is the responsibility of both teacher and parent to remain in constant contact and seek alternative methods of discipline to make the student successful.

Expected answers:

"I build relationships with my students."

"I teach students our classroom expectations, routines, and procedures."

"I reinforce positive behavior."

"I am organized and allow students very little idle time."

"I work with parents."

"I attempt to resolve student issues inside of the classroom."

"I seek alternative methods to get students to perform."

27

Think Like a Teacher, Act Like a Parent

Unacceptable answers:

"I send students to the office."

"I write their names on the board for detention or missed recess."

What to do if the teacher gives an unacceptable answer:

- Talk with the teacher.

- Schedule monthly meetings with the teacher and your child.

- Create behavior charts for your child to have signed by the teacher.

Chapter 1: Think Like a Teacher

Parent Centered Questions

Question 5

What can I do to ensure my child is able to take accelerated classes? What are the qualifications and deadlines for the honors program? Is my child on track to take part in honors preparation courses?

Purpose of the question:

Education is our society's greatest equalizer and it is the key to upward social mobility. It is honorable to desire for your child to not only to attend school but also to accelerate. Much like our society, by design our schools create levels or *tracks* which lead students to certain career/life opportunities. The practice of tracking is quite simple and happens very early in education.

Redbirds vs. Bluebirds

Let's say there are two reading groups in kindergarten, the "bluebirds" and the "redbirds." This type of thing seems innocent to the naked eye, but in reality, the bluebird group are the advanced readers. Generally speaking, they receive a more challenging reading curriculum and will continue to excel at rates much greater than the redbirds.

While the redbirds are not totally neglected, their work will consist of supportive activities rather than challenging activities. (Note to parents: It is essential for you to work with your child at home every day to provide challenge and support.) As these same students continue their educational careers, the bluebirds will continue to receive advanced work. As time goes on, this gap between the educational haves and have-nots continues to widen. Once a student is placed on a track, moving to a higher track is often virtually impossible, which is the most harmful part of

29

Think Like a Teacher, Act Like a Parent

the tracking process. In most schools, if a student is not on the honors, gifted, or accelerated track by the 4th grade, they will never have the opportunity to catch/move up. Fast-forward to their twelfth grade year. The bluebird is taking College Algebra and receiving college credit, while the redbird is two or three years behind taking high school geometry. Now ask yourself: Which student has the better life opportunities?

Don't believe this is an issue? Notice the track of classes that teacher's children, wealthy children, and politically connected families generally take. Every school has some sort of accelerated curriculum. It may be referred to as Honors, Advanced Placement (AP), Gifted, Bluebirds, etc. Do not let the teacher, principal, or anyone else in the school act as though they are unaware of such practices.

Expected answers:

"Here are the expectations for our accelerated courses." (Brochure, pamphlet, website, etc.)

"To get on the honors track, students need to read _____ amount of words; your child is almost there. I will send you extra exercises to see if we can make him/her ready to move up."

Chapter 1: Think Like a Teacher

Unacceptable answers:

"We teach all of our students the exact same." (If that were the case, then where are the children that already know the information?)

"There's no more room in the accelerated courses."

"Sorry, you just missed the deadline."

"The only way into the program is to be recommended by a teacher."

What to do if the teacher gives an unacceptable answer:

- Make sure your student is academically prepared for the higher track and be prepared to prove this.

- Speak with her/his teacher.

- Speak with the principal, superintendent, or curriculum coordinator.

- If you must, contact an attorney specializing in education or a specialized educational advocate.

Think Like a Teacher, Act Like a Parent

Question 6

How does my child learn, and how can I best support him at home?

Purpose of the question:
Chances are your child's teacher spends more time with your child than you do. Since teachers are trained experts in the area of education, they should have some idea within the first few weeks of school what type of learning style works best for your child. The term Multiple Intelligences implies that every student is intelligent and able to learn if the lesson is presented in a way that caters to their specific style. A skilled teacher will pick up on your child's learning style.

Much like every other component in this book, the teacher is not alone in this process: YOU have the greatest responsibility. I suggest telling the teacher your child's areas of strength and how your child learns.

For example, my five year old son loves to learn. He is a mixture between an auditory learner and kinesthetic learner. He enjoys movement and is very social. He does not like art. Prior to his starting school, we created his personal "résumé" and gave it to his teacher.

Remember, there may be 25 other students in the class. The teacher cannot teach only your child's preference. However, a good teacher teaches with differentiated instruction, providing the same lesson several different ways. Teachers are required to attend classes, workshops, and trainings to perfect this skill.

32

Chapter 1: Think Like a Teacher

Expected answers:

> "From what I can tell, your child learns best by doing projects."

> "Shaun has already mastered _____ skill. To better support him, you should encourage him to practice _____ skill twenty minutes per day."

> "Here is a list of websites, apps for your tablet, and books. If you need more, let me know, and I will try to run a few extra copies for you."

Unacceptable answers:

> "Since there are so many students in class, I do not have the opportunity to teach each student in the way they learn."

> "Differentiated instruction is something those younger teachers do. I don't believe it's really important."

What to do if the teacher gives an unacceptable answer:

- Document the attempt to discuss this matter.

- Speak with the principal.

- Continue advocating for your child.

- Continue working with your child at home.

*Again, ultimately your child is your responsibility

Think Like a Teacher, Act Like a Parent

How Does My Child Learn?

Determining learning styles is not an exact science. However, the inventory below will help you better understand how your child learns. This sample learning assessment is very basic. I encourage you to seek a more detailed assessment that offers clearer results and recommendations. I have provided such an assessment at http://www.weteachparents.com.

Learning Style Inventory (SAMPLE)

Place a check in the appropriate space after each statement below. Then use the scoring directions at the bottom of the page to evaluate your responses. This 24-item survey should not be timed. (Respond to each statement as honestly as you can. Remember, there are no incorrect answers and honesty will benefit your child.)

34

Chapter 1: Think Like a Teacher

	Often	Sometimes	Seldom
1. I can remember things best by listening to the teacher's explanations and class discussions.			X
2. I like to see information written on the board, reading out of the book, and also looking at visual aids.		X	
3. I like to write things down or to take notes for visual review.	X		
4. I prefer to make posters, models, or actual practice and other activities in class.	X		
5. I need explanations of diagrams, graphs, or visual directions.		X	
6. I enjoy working with my hands or making things.	X		
7. I am skillful with and enjoy developing and making graphs and charts.		X	
8. I can tell if sounds match when presented with pairs of sounds.	X		
9. I can remember best by writing things down.		X	
10. I easily understand and follow directions on a map.	X		
11. I do best in class by listening.		X	
12. I play with coins or keys in my pocket.	X		
13. I learn to spell better by repeating words out loud than by writing the words on paper.		X	
14. I can understand a news article better by reading about it in a newspaper than by listening to a report about it.	X		

35

Think Like a Teacher, Act Like a Parent

15. I chew gum and snack while studying.	X		
16. I think the best way to remember something is to picture it in your head.		X	
17. I learn the spelling of words by "finger spelling" them.		X	
18. I would rather listen to a speech than read about the same material in a textbook.			X
19. I am good at solving jigsaw puzzles and mazes.		X	
20. I grip objects in my hands during learning periods.	X		
21. I prefer listening to the news on the radio rather than reading the paper.		X	
22. I would rather get information about an interesting subject by reading about it.	X		
23. I feel very comfortable touching others, hugging, handshaking, etc.	X		
24. I follow oral directions better than written ones.			X

Chapter 1: Think Like a Teacher

Scoring

Directions: Place the point value on the line next to the corresponding item below. Add the points in each column to obtain the preference score under each heading.

OFTEN = 5 points, SOMETIMES = 3 points, SELDOM = 1 points

VISUAL (Seeing)		AUDITORY (Listening)		KINESETHETIC (Touching)	
NO.	PTS.	NO.	PTS.	NO.	PTS.
2	3	1	1	4	5
3	5	5	3	6	5
7	3	8	5	9	3
10	5	11	3	12	5
14	5	13	3	15	5
16	3	18	1	17	3
19	3	21	3	20	5
22	5	24	1	23	5
VPS =	**33**	**APS =**	**20**	**TPS =**	**36**

Think Like a Teacher, Act Like a Parent

Characteristics of Learning Styles

Three of your senses are mainly used in learning and recalling information. Your eyes, ears, and sense of touch play essential roles in the way you communicate, perceive reality, and relate to others. Because you learn and communicate best with others that share your learning style, it is important to know and take advantage your individual strengths. Below are a few signs that may help you determine your child's learning style.

Visual:

- Mind sometimes strays during verbal activities
- Observe rather than acts or talks
- Likes to read
- Usually a good speller
- Memorizes by seeing graphics or pictures
- Remembers faces
- Meticulous, neat in appearance

Auditory:

- Talks to self aloud
- Enjoys talking
- Enjoys music
- Whispers to self while reading
- Distracted by noise
- Hums or sings
- Enjoys listening activities

Chapter 1: Think Like a Teacher

Kinesthetic:

- In motion most of the time
- Likes to touch people when talking
- Taps pencil or foot when studying
- Enjoys doing activities
- Likes to solve problems by physically working through them
- Will try new things
- Outgoing by nature

SOUND: Hints for the Auditory Learner

General

1. Speak the information aloud.
2. Read into a tape recorder and replay it.
3. Have someone read the information to you.

Reading/Writing

1. Plan each sentence you want to write by saying it aloud or silently in your head.
2. Say each sentence several times.
3. Write each sentence as you say it, or talk into a tape recorder, dictating each sentence of your paragraph; then play the tape back – one sentence at a time – and record your paragraph in writing.

Think Like a Teacher, Act Like a Parent

Mathematics

1. Learn math while saying the concept, fact, theorem, etc., aloud.
2. Explain math problems, concepts, facts, etc. to yourself by relating the information out loud.
3. Use a tape recorder and replay the information.

SIGHT: Hints for the Visual Learner

General

1. Take notes, make pictures, graphs, and charts. Use flashcards that highlight key details (include pictures).
2. Sit close to the teacher so that you can watch his /her face and gestures.
3. Record homework assignments in a date book, on a note pad, or a specially designed assignment sheet.

Reading/Writing

1. Use sight words, flashcards, note cards, and experience stories; don't try to sound words out, but try to determine if the new word or words includes terms you already know. For example, the word "systematic" has the words "system", "stem," and "mat" within it.
2. You are a "look-and-say" learner. Look at a word carefully, and then say it.

40

Chapter 1: Think Like a Teacher

Mathematics

1. Visualize the problem.
2. Make pictures or tallies of the problem on scratch paper.
3. Write the problem.

TOUCH: Hints for the Kinesthetic Learner

General

1. Keep your desk clear of distracting objects. Distractions will ruin you.
2. Cover the page you're not reading
3. If you are distracted by noise, turn off the radio; wear earplugs or headphones to block out the noise. If you want sound, listen to soft music.

Reading/Writing

1. Create outline of ideas.
2. Write about real life experiences.
3. Complete work in a stimulating, non-disruptive environment.

Mathematics

1. Use tangible items to figure out mathematic problems.
2. Play mathematic games. (Example: Various Card Games)
3. Count using number lines.

Think Like a Teacher, Act Like a Parent

Carter "Doc" Hardy

2015 School Year

1234 Fifth St.
Yourtown, USA 54321
weteachchildren@gmail.com
@weteachchildren

My mom's name is Nicole Hardy, and my dad's name is Carter Hardy. I also have a sister named Olivia Hardy. Our phone number is **555-555-5555.** You can call them anytime.

OBJECTIVES
When I grow-up I want to be a doctor, a ninja, a chef, and the president.

EDUCATION
Ms. Pickadilly's Kindergarten
Central School #72
Reading Level 2.6
Math Level 2.0

INTERESTS
Karate
Notre Dame Football
Power Rangers

I AM REALLY GOOD AT:
Computers
Reading

Chapter 1: Think Like a Teacher

Olivia "Live" Hardy

2015 School Year

1234 Fifth St.
Yourtown, USA 54321
weteachparents@gmail.com
@weteachparents

My granny's name is Louise Hardy, and my grandpa's name is Carter Hardy. I also have a brother named Carter Hardy. Our phone number is **555-555-5555.** You can call them anytime.

OBJECTIVES
When I grow-up I want to be a teacher, an animal doctor, a quilt maker, and a cookie baker.

EDUCATION
Ms. Ellen's Pre-K
Little Learners Preschool Academy
Reading Level K.7
Math Level K.9

INTERESTS
Gymnastics and dance
Animals
Helping mom cook

I AM REALLY GOOD AT:
Computers and tablets
Math

Think Like a Teacher, Act Like a Parent

Question 7

How can I help/support the classroom?

Purpose of the question:
Students perform better when their parents are actively involved. If you believe in the power of education and want to ensure your child has the best life opportunities beyond high school, GET INVOLVED. Schools are usually huge places and need lots of help they simply can't afford. Just read your local paper. How many times in the past year have you read or heard about "financial cut-backs" being made at the local school? You may not be a teacher, but you can certainly help support the teachers that you are entrusting with your children. Below is a list of ways you may be able to help:

1. Shelve books in the library
2. Hang pictures
3. Move boxes
4. Cut out shapes to be used in class
5. Staple papers
6. Chaperone dances and activities
7. Volunteer coach
8. Donate snacks and supplies
9. Serve on parent committees
10. Serve on the school board
11. Talk with students on career day
12. Join the Parent-Teacher group (PTO, PTA, PTSA)

There are thousands of other ways you can assist the school (and therefore assist your student). The most important thing is your presence. Your presence alone will ensure your child, the teachers, and even the principal are all aligned in the educational process.

Chapter 1: Think Like a Teacher

Schools want parents involved. Do your research: The highest performing schools have the highest parental involvement. In fact, many private schools insist that parents sign contracts and pledge a certain level of involvement.

*Note: Most schools have specific protocols for volunteers to follow. You may be asked to complete some kind of background check. Understandably, schools must be careful not to allow criminals and predators around our precious children. Also, some schools do not allow parents to volunteer in their child's classroom. The reason for this is sometimes parents become more of a distraction than help. Even if you cannot work directly in your child's classroom, just your being at the school will make a difference.

Expected answers (from a happy teacher):
"Oh my, I would love some extra help. Here is a list of classroom tasks you might be interested in."

"Great! Please go to the office and fill out the volunteer information form."

Unacceptable answers:
"I usually don't like the parents to be around."

"Our school does not use volunteers."

Think Like a Teacher, Act Like a Parent

What to do if you receive an unacceptable answer:

- First, do an internal audit. Be honest with yourself. Is there something in your background that may prevent you from working with children?

- Keep asking and being persistent. If the teacher says no, then ask the librarian. If he says no, ask the principal. If she says no, form or join the PTA (Parent Teacher Association). If that does not work, run for the school board. I am sure you will not have to go this far. At most schools, the "harvest is plentiful, but the laborers are few."

Chapter 1: Think Like a Teacher

Question 8

Does my child seem happy at school?

Purpose of the question:

School is going to be a permanent part of your child's life for many years. Students spend approximately eight hours per day at school for five days a week. While many adults spend the same amount of time at jobs they do not like, they have the choice of leaving. Though some may feel students need to "just deal with" their issues at school, this isn't really a practical, viable option. School is one of the places that teach children coping skills. The ability and method a child uses to cope with a problem is important. If a child miserable at school can easily become depressed. It is important to find the reason for a child's discomfort and address it immediately. Is the child being teased? Is the teacher being unfair? Is something at home affecting the child? Is the work too hard? Are there processing or sensory issues? Whatever the reason, a parent may not be aware of their child's disposition at school, but should do everything in their power to figure it out.

Expected answers:

"I will keep a closer eye on him and report to you what I am seeing."

"Do you have any suggestions for clubs/organizations he may want to join?"

"Our school has a behavior analysis collection sheet. This form tracks student behavior. Would you like for me to track his behavior and report it to you?"

47

Think Like a Teacher, Act Like a Parent

"We have a Pupil Support Team (PST) that discusses student needs and creates interventions specific to the student. Do you mind if I mention him to our PST?"

Unacceptable answers:

"Due to the demands of the curriculum, I am unable to pay close attention to student's emotional needs."

"Kids will be kids... they have their ups and downs. This is probably just a phase, and given some time he/she will get over it.

What to do if the teacher gives an unacceptable answer:

- Talk with your child.

- Ask to speak with the school counselor or social worker.

- Make sure your child is involved with afterschool group activities they enjoy and allows them to experience success. (i.e. Boy/Girl Scouts, Karate, Band, Athletic Teams, Dance Team, Computer Club)

Maslow's Hierarchy of Needs

While preparing to become teachers, educators are taught the importance of teaching the "whole child." Teaching is more than just following the prescribed curriculum. To make students productive members of society, we must understand that children have needs aside from the information in their textbooks. Abraham Maslow, a psychologist known for developing the hierarchy of needs, gives educators a framework by which to address the "whole child." Working from the bottom of the pyramid to the top, Maslow shows that for students to be their best, certain needs must be met:

Think Like a Teacher, Act Like a Parent

- At the most basic level, students need food, water, and shelter.

- Students need to be safe and free of fear in a stable learning environment.

- Students must feel a sense of love and belonging. At school, this includes participation in clubs, activities, and organizations.

- Self-esteem is essential to the learning process. Teachers must spend time teaching students the importance of a positive self-image and high self-esteem.

- When the needs of students are being met, he or she is at their best and can pursue/fulfill their need to be creative and add to society.

Chapter 1: Think Like a Teacher

Student Centered Questions

Question 9

By the end of the year, what is my child expected to know and where is he/she now? How will my child's progress be measured and reported to me?

Purpose of the question:
Our educational system's primary functions are to increase the student's knowledge base while guiding their curiosity toward new and innovative solutions. Both public and private schools have teaching guides, curriculum maps, or some kind of "road map" detailing what students should know by the end of the year. When aspiring teachers are in college, they are taught to make lesson plans. Every lesson plan has the statement, "By the end of the lesson, the students will be able to..."

As a parent, you should start each year with the end in mind. "What should my student know at the end of the day, week, year?"

Teaching plans are dictated by state and federal standards which are not variable. Teachers choose how to teach, but not what to teach. Do not compare today's education to yours! Just because you learned cursive in the third grade does not mean it is part of today's curriculum.

Once the teaching has taken place, the teacher must assess the student's learning. The most traditional method of assessment is by giving some type of exam. I am sure you remember multiple choice, true/false, and short answer formats. Exams are one of many ways to assess student learning. Other and more preferred methods

51

Think Like a Teacher, Act Like a Parent

include student projects, labs, reports, and in-class debates. These methods not only assess the student's ability to remember the information, but their ability to synthesize, evaluate and apply the information to real life circumstances.

Schools monitor the progress of every student. Traditional monitoring includes report cards, progress reports, etc. However, progress monitoring has come a long way since you were a child. Today there are many new methods to monitor your child's progress. Progress monitoring is the responsibility of both the parent and the teacher. Many schools subscribe to gradebook communication services, such as TeacherEase or Skyward. These systems allow parents to monitor their child's progress daily. As teachers input grades, parents receive emails and notices of assignments due, assignments completed, and many other important communications about the child's academic well-being. You should check this at least twice per week. These great systems prevent surprises. They also prevent students from intercepting bad reports or changing grades, thus making sure a well-connected parent is always in the loop.

Expected answers:

"I follow the curriculum guide adopted by our school/district. You can access this on our school's website, or if you like, I can provide you with a copy."

"I monitor progress by doing group and individual projects, giving exams, daily in-class assignments, homework, and group discussions."

52

Chapter 1: Think Like a Teacher

"I update grades every Monday, Wednesday, and Fridays. You can access his/her grades anytime on our grade communication system."

Unacceptable answers:

"I kind of teach what I think they should know."

"Grades are determined solely by the tests I administer at the end of each chapter."

"I only put grades in my grade book. I do not use the computer grade book communication system."

What to do if the teacher gives an unacceptable answer:

- Let the teacher know you are very interested in updates a minimum of once per week. If the teacher forgets or fails to update you, make sure you follow through with your request.

- Contact the teacher and carbon copy the principal on your request (via the textbox labeled "CC" in most email programs/services). If you are still not getting what you are requesting, speak with the principal directly.

Think Like a Teacher, Act Like a Parent

Question 10

What systems are in place to respond to my child's social and emotional needs?

Purpose of the question:
Schools are responsible for educating the "whole child." This goes beyond reading, writing, and arithmetic; the school must assist the student in becoming a better person and a productive part of society. Children are humans at their peak of immaturity: filled with energy and lacking direction; apt to having scuffles on the playground; and prone to gossip, rumors, and hurt feelings.

Schools are responsible for teaching students healthy coping skills and strategies. You may have heard of programs such as Character Counts, Positive Behavior Interventions and Supports (PBIS), Positive Behavior Facilitation (PBF), the Nurtured Heart Approach, and many, many more. I am not suggesting one program over the other. I am, suggesting you become familiar with the program your child's school uses and ask the teacher about the program. Teasing, fighting, and bullying are unfortunate realities of childhood. Many problems stem from an interaction at school. If such interactions are caught early enough, our schools and children might be a little safer and a little happier. Character education programs may not stop all of our society's ills, but I have witnessed their effectiveness in many schools.

Chapter 1: Think Like a Teacher

Expected answers:

"We use the _____ character education curriculum."

"We have regular class discussions, lessons, and assemblies about social issues."

Unacceptable answers:

"I only teach science. I am not responsible for raising someone else's child."

"Our school does not have a formal plan for support."

"We discuss social issues on a case-by-case basis."

What to do if you receive an unacceptable answer:

- Research various programs and suggest them to the teacher, principal, and superintendent.

- Volunteer to start such a program or serve on a school committee for character education.

- Attend a school board meeting and brag on a neighboring school which incorporates character education.

Think Like a Teacher, Act Like a Parent

Question 11
Is my child working to his/her best ability?

Purpose of the question:
The purpose of this question — much like the purpose of this book — is to create complete transparency within the educational system. Keep in mind, rather than playing a game of "gotcha" with the teacher, you are trying to ensure your child receives the best possible education. All parties involved share this burden. Parents and teachers are responsible for setting the stage by removing all excuses and distractions. Children are responsible for receiving the educational services offered by the school. Since their personal potential is not quantifiable, we rely on teachers to stretch our children beyond their academic limits.

For example, Jack and Jill are twins who have the same teacher for math class. Jill is somewhat lazy, but has a more natural ability in mathematics. Jack, however, is a hard worker. Jack tries hard yet only earns a C+ in math, while Jill puts forth little effort and earns a B+. Which would you rather? Personally, I would rather Jack's C+. Though Jill earned a higher grade, how much did she truly learn?

Let's go beyond the grade. Many times a grade represents the retention of information. This is a great skill and commendable in many circumstances. However, effort is a skill which is transferable to life beyond the classroom. Though his grade is a note lower, Jack's hard work and attempts to gain a greater understanding shows he values education and the application of knowledge. Again, education is not only about the retaining and regurgitation of information; it is about analyzing, evaluating, and

56

Chapter 1: Think Like a Teacher

synthesizing information to create independent and creative thinkers. Further, we should always seek out skills which are transferable beyond the four walls of the classroom.

Explain to your child's teacher you are concerned about their letter grades, but you are much more interested in maximizing your child's potential. Getting an A+ is not good enough. The teacher and curriculum must be as rigorous as possible. Keep in mind your child is not only competing with the other students in the class, but is in constant competition with children all over the world. While at this point in their lives, this competition may not seem important, it sets the stage for "real world" competitiveness your child is sure to face when seeking further education, employment, and even social status.

Expected answers:

"Jack is working very hard and doing well. We will continue to challenge him and let you know his progress."

"Since Jill already understands the concepts in this unit, we are allowing her to work ahead at a pace that is comfortable for her. Some of her lessons she does independently on the computer."

"We are giving Jill a few additional assignments. She is learning the same concepts as the rest of the class. However, the work we are giving Jill is providing her with a deeper understanding and a greater challenge."

Think Like a Teacher, Act Like a Parent

Unacceptable answers:

"I'm not really sure. With 25 students in my class, it is hard to tell who is working to their potential."

"I treat all the students the same. The curriculum will not allow any additional challenges for students that already understand."

"Jill got an A. She is so smart. She's doing just fine."

What to do if you receive an unacceptable answer:

- Talk with your child alone and then in-conference with the teacher. Let your child know their greatest effort is expected. Also reassure them that an earned C+ trumps an easy A.

- Talk with the teacher and let her know the goal is not only an A grade. Rather, you desire a rigorous and challenging education for your child. You want your child to learn and not just show what they already know.

- Ask the teacher and principal about additional opportunities for enrichment. Schools are filled with brilliant children not being challenged by the traditional curriculum. What academic enrichment opportunities exist in the school and within the school community?

58

Chapter 1: Think Like a Teacher

Individualized Student Success Plan

Student's Name: _____ **Grade:** _____

Subject: _____

Goals & Grades:

Weeks	Goals	Grades
1-3		
4-6		
6-9		

(*Most schools formally report grades every 9 weeks. The purpose of a success plan is to ensure students are keeping up with the curriculum and that their skill sets are appropriate to build upon. For this reason, grades are consistently monitored and reported in 3-week intervals. Consistent reporting holds students, parents, and teachers accountable for the success of the student.)

Specific Concerns:

Which specific skill sets/taught concepts have not been mastered by the student?

_____

_____

_____

Think Like a Teacher, Act Like a Parent

Suggested Instructional Adjustments:
How can the teacher differentiate instruction to meet the student's learning style?

_____

_____

_____

Suggested Curricular Adjustments:
Is the curriculum relevant, purposeful, and appropriate for the student?

_____

_____

_____

Suggested Environmental Adjustments:
Is the learning environment conducive for learning? What changes can be made specific to the needs of this student?

_____

_____

_____

Chapter 1: Think Like a Teacher

Other Targeted Interventions:

_____ **Pull-out Tutoring**

_____ **Mentoring**

_____ **Computer-based Instruction**

_____ **Behavior Contract**

_____ **Student Success Center**

_____ **Social Work**

_____ **Extended Test Time**

_____ **Homework Club**

Next 3 Meeting Dates:

Parent   Teacher

Student

*Please attach a copy of the parent-teacher contact log

Think Like a Teacher, Act Like a Parent

My Goal for This Week

This Week's Goal Must be SMART
(**S**pecific, **M**easurable, **A**ssignable, **R**ealistic, and **T**imed)

My goal for this week is:

_____

_____

_____

I met this goal because:

_____

_____

_____

To meet this goal next week I will:

_____

_____

_____

_____

(Student)   (Parent)

_____

(Teacher)

62

Chapter 2:
Act Like a Parent

Years ago there was a television show called *Kids Say the Darndest Things*. In essence, the host asked a group of children a series of questions and awaited their brutally honest responses. Though we laughed at the answers, many times the children provided us with their views of the world.

Understanding how your child feels about school is important. Consider this: Your child spends up to 40 hours per week at school. Schools play a major role in raising and shaping our children. Have you ever been in a situation where you tell your child one thing and your child informs you that you are wrong because the teacher said the opposite? Children learn a lot from school, and no matter how much we think we know or how many questions we ask the teacher, the best way to find out what is really going on at school is by talking and **listening** to our children.

As with the previous section, this list of questions and concerns is not exhaustive. It is a starting point. Your child should be able to answer the following questions. From these answers, you should gain insight into their life at school. Also included in this section are a few resources to ensure you maximize your parenting abilities.

Think Like a Teacher, Act Like a Parent

<u>School Centered Questions</u>

Question 12

Can you teach me what you learned today?

Purpose of the question:
Notice the wording of this question is not "tell" me what you learned but "**teach**" me what you learned. The purpose of this question is quite simple. The highest form of learning is teaching! If your child can teach you what they learned in school then there's no doubt they paid attention to the lesson, understood it, and can apply it to real life situations. Further, children enjoy "knowing something you don't know."

Expected answer:
(Extremely Happy Child!) "Okay let me show you!"

*Of course, if you already know the lesson/answer, act as if you do not. If they ask questions, get a few of them wrong and let your child teach you and find alternative ways to make you understand. This will build their ability to think independently and creatively.

Unacceptable answers:
"We didn't do anything today."

"I can't remember."

64

Chapter 2: Act Like a Parent

What to do if you receive an unacceptable answer:

- Consult the class calendar.

- Review your child's homework.

- Contact the teacher and ask for weekly calendar of lesson subjects.

- Create fun learning and review games for your child.

*There are thousands of ideas on the internet. Check sites like Google, Pinterest, Yahoo, Bing… just search for "fun learning" ideas and pick your favorites.

Think Like a Teacher, Act Like a Parent

Ten Words your Student Must Know to Perform Well on Tests!

1	compare	tell how things are alike
2	contrast	tell how things are different
3	describe	tell how something looks, sounds, and feels
4	diagram	explain using lines, a web, or other graphic organization
5	evaluate	give your opinion about the value of a topic
6	explain	tell what something means or how something works
7	identify	answer the "5 Ws" and H (who, what, when, where, why, and how) about a topic
8	illustrate	show how something works by using examples
9	prove	present facts that show something is true
10	summarize	tell just the key information about a topic

Chapter 2: Act Like a Parent

Question 13

Where is your homework? Tell me about your homework.

Purpose of the question:

Again, notice the wording of the question. Do not ask "if" there is homework, but rather ask "where" is the homework. Think back to when you were a child. If your parent asked if you had homework, chances are the answer was a resounding, "No!" By asking where the homework is, your child knows you expect them to do something educational at home on a daily basis. Homework does not have to be lengthy, but it must be expected.

If the teacher does not give homework, your child should have a library book to read, an educational computer game, or even an education app on their tablet. As a parent, it is necessary for you to have something in place to ensure your child practices educational skills at school and at home.

Expected answers:

"I have math homework. I did some of it at school, but I have a few more problems to finish."

"The teacher did not give us any, but I have my reading book."

"Can I play with the math app on the tablet?"

Unacceptable answers:

"I don't have any. The teacher did not give us any homework."

"I did it all during free time/study hall."

Think Like a Teacher, Act Like a Parent

What to do if you receive an unacceptable answer:

- Ask the teacher for additional work.

- Double-check your child's assignment notebook.

- Go to the library, and let them pick out any book to read.

*Remember, though schools provide education, your job is to mandate education. Do not wait for your child's teacher to put their minds to work. There are plenty of websites, apps, workbooks and libraries available. Further, many of the aforementioned resources are available free of charge. Schools are great, but they cannot do everything. As a parent, you must step up and provide your student with learning opportunities, even if the school does not.

Chapter 2: Act Like a Parent

Question 14

What is the coolest thing your teacher does? Explain more. What do you like best about school?

Purpose of the question:
School may not be your child's favorite place in the world, but something cool happens there. The purpose of this question is twofold. First, by speaking positive about schools we shape the opinions of our children. It is popular for a child to act as if they do not like school. When in reality, children love school. How do I know? Halfway into summer vacation, ask your child if they are ready to go back to school. Schools are fun at least part of the time. Just imagine if you and all of your friends worked at the same place and spent all day together? Though deep down every child may feel it, we certainly want them to think and say there is something special and enjoyable about school.

Secondly, asking this question allows you to view the teacher through your child's eyes. How does the teacher reach the students? Is the teacher creative? Is the teacher friendly? Is the teacher consistent? (And on and on and on.) Trust me. If you just ask, your child will tell you everything you want to know and much more.

Think Like a Teacher, Act Like a Parent

Expected answers (Your child should become an absolute chatter-box)**:**

>"She lets us play learning games."

>"He dresses up like silly characters."

>"She lets us choose partners when we work in centers."

>"She always smiles at us."

Unacceptable answers:

>"Nothing."

>"I don't know."

What to do if you receive an unacceptable answer:

- Keep asking, probing, and prying. Do not let your child dodge this question. Finding out what they like about their teacher and what they like about school is essential to their success.

- If they really do not like *anything* about school, I suggest digging deeper into their life. This is a sign that something else may be wrong (i.e. depression, bullying, poor grades, social anxiety, etc.)

- If there is a problem with the teacher be sure to schedule an appointment to speak with the teacher, school counselor, and/or the principal.

70

Chapter 2: Act Like a Parent

Question 15

What do you do when you don't understand the teacher's directions?

Purpose of the question:
Your child is likely to be in class with 20-30 other children. The job of the teacher includes reviewing, assessing, and presenting new information. This may sound like an easy job on the surface, but realistically teaching children is a very challenging job. There will be times when the teacher is presenting information faster than your child's ability to process it, or maybe your child was out ill and missed the previous day's lesson. With 20 plus students in the classroom, it is challenging to provide individual instruction, especially when a student does not ask for help.

Children must "own" their education and learn to self-advocate. The old cliché states "the squeaky wheel gets the oil." This holds true in education. Teachers are guided by curriculum timelines and work at challenging paces to present the most material possible within a given timeframe. If your child does understand or does not "get it," then it is their responsibility to ask the teacher to slow down, re-explain, or provide additional examples. This form of self-advocating will ensure they get the most out of their educational experiences.

Self-advocating is an important education and life skill. As children grow older, they become more image conscious and stop asking for help because they do not want to "look dumb." Parents must empower their children to ask questions and reassure them that there is no such thing as a bad question. Additionally, it is your responsibility to ask

71

Think Like a Teacher, Act Like a Parent

questions of your child and the teacher. Education is a world of its own and has a language of its own. Just as with your child, if the teacher says something you do not understand, ask for clarity and keep asking until you have a complete understanding. We are talking about your child's life. One decision made at school can guide your child's academic, professional, and personal life for eternity. Schools use lots of specific terms, and you'd **better** know what they mean!

Expected answers:
"I ask the teacher for more help."

"I go to lunchtime tutoring."

"I ask the teacher for help during study hall."

"I ask Jill for help. She always has the right answers."

Unacceptable answers:
"I don't say anything. I don't want to look stupid!"

"I just sit there. I think the teacher knows I need help."

"I just try to keep going without any help."

Chapter 2: Act Like a Parent

What to do if you receive an unacceptable answer:

- Talk with your child about self-advocating and practice ways to ask for help.

- Talk with the teacher to see if they notice any problem with your child during the lessons.

- Create a plan for your child to ask for help in a non-interrupting manner (i.e. if your child needs help, they can discreetly place a red pencil on the edge of the desk so the teacher knows to walk over and provide additional assistance).

- Remind your child that they have dreams and the only way to accomplish those dreams is by getting a good education.

- Continue promoting your child's self-esteem.

Think Like a Teacher, Act Like a Parent

Peer Centered Questions

Question 16

How do you feel when someone is being mean towards you? How often do you do what your friends want instead of what you want? When you look in the mirror, what do you see?

Purpose of the question:

I realize this is more than one question, but asking these questions will help you interpret your child's self-esteem! Self-esteem refers to the way your child sees, thinks and feels about themself. Just think of your personal experiences with self-esteem. Do you have a healthy concept of who you are? What does your inner voice tell you? How do you deal with your personal victories and defeats? How do you make sure you are your best self on a daily basis?

You should know, or try to find out, what your child thinks about themself. High self-esteem and self-confidence are necessary for a student to be successful in life and education. Michael Grose, a popular parent coach states, "Self-esteem is a greater predictor of a child's success than intellectual ability or natural talent." A student may master all the skills needed to do well in any subject area; however, if the student does not believe he or she is capable of doing the work, the student's chances of success decrease tremendously. Students with high self-esteem are more likely to make positive friendships, persevere through difficult situations, become problem-solvers, excel in school, and are less likely to be victims of bullying.

In contrast, students with poor self-esteem and lower self-confidence are often shy and struggle to develop

74

Chapter 2: Act Like a Parent

friendships. Many times, they underachieve in school, lack coping skills and suffer from depression, are easily influenced by others, and are targeted by bullies.

Your child's self-esteem may be determined by achievement in four areas:
- Social (family, friendships, acceptance)

- Competence (in a skill area)

- Physical (appearance, clothing, accepted by peers and family)

- Character (effort, generosity, etc.)

Ultimately, it is your responsibility to make sure your child feels good about themselves. Luckily, it's easy to add a few "tools in your belt" to assist and shape your child's self-image.

Your child's self-esteem will fluctuate as they grow and experience new things. Please don't be alarmed or panicked if your child is not happy for a day or two.

Expected answers:
"When someone is mean to me I feel sad or angry."

"I walk away and stop playing with those kids."

"I get away from the kid and go tell Ms. Green."

"Sometimes I do what my friends want to do, and sometimes they do what I want to do. We take turns and share."

Think Like a Teacher, Act Like a Parent

Unacceptable answers:

"When someone is being mean I feel very sad. I feel like I have to let them be mean to me so they will like me."

"I do what my friends want to do all the time because I don't want them to be mad at me and not be my friends."

What to do if you receive an unacceptable answer:

- If you suspect your child is suffering from low self-esteem, the first thing you should do is take advantage of your school's resources. Contact the school counselor/social worker and schedule a meeting to explain your concerns. Ask your school counselor/social worker if they have a social-skills group your child can join to help increase their self-esteem.

- Counseling groups are good for students who struggle with low self-esteem. Being part of a group gives students a sense of belonging, helps them realize they are not the only student that experiences these feelings, and provides them an opportunity to learn how to cope with different situations and feelings from their peers. Also, ask if the school counselor/social worker can meet with your child once a week for at least a month to determine if your child's low self-esteem is a sign of a greater issue, such as depression, and if you should seek professional help outside of the school. Don't panic if your school does not offer social and emotional groups or resources for students. In your community, there are mental health organizations that offer groups for adolescents. A second step is to

Chapter 2: Act Like a Parent

provide opportunities for your child to have positive experiences. Try to involve your child with activities in the community. Camps, sports through your local park district, church youth groups, scout troops, YMCA programs, and even martial arts can all be great self-confidence boosters!

Think Like a Teacher, Act Like a Parent

Question 17

Which of your friends do you think I like the best? Why?

Purpose of the question:
The old adage, "Birds of a feather flock together," is certainly true. As an educator, I have heard many parents claim that their child was "following the wrong crowd." I hate to say it, but often children are **not** following the wrong crowd, but they are actually part of the crowd. It is difficult and maybe even impossible to pick your child's friends. However, you can control their exposure to certain people, places, events, and ideas. If your child's only heroes are on television, then expect them to seek similar attributes when they search for friends. Every child needs to choose from multiple realities. Take your child to museums, ball games, church, plays, etc. Teach them about people important to your culture and personal history. Reinforce that certain people are cool and certain behaviors are unacceptable. Be the person you want your child to be. Just think about your parents. Chances are when you became an adult you became a very similar to them, even if you always swore you never would.

Be sure to meet your child's friends and their parents if at all possible. This may become a bit more difficult as children get older, but if you are a solid role model, they will revert to your good attributes as they get older. As with school, set a high standard and expect your child to reach this standard. Your child is the crowd! *(I regularly provide students with the following scenario and question: If you are in a car and your buddy robs a bank and gets in the car with you... Who goes to jail? Answer: Everyone in the car!)*

Chapter 2: Act Like a Parent

Expected answers:

"Nina is my best friend because we play together at recess."

"Shaun is my best friend because he helps me during group time."

Unacceptable answers:

"Robbie is funny. In class he burps loud like SpongeBob."

"I like Cheyanne because she makes the class laugh when the teacher is talking."

What to do if you receive an unacceptable answer:

- Talk with your child about your behavioral expectations.

- Teach your child about your family history and how to respect it.

- Request your child's seat to be moved.

- Step in, only if necessary, but be careful. There may be pushback.

Think Like a Teacher, Act Like a Parent

Question 18

Which school club/activity do you plan to join?

Purpose of the question:

A great way educators keep students engaged in school is by offering a wide variety of extra-curricular activities. It is not possible for a school to know the interests of every student, but it is easy for the parent to know the interest of their child. Once you know the interest of your child, it is your responsibility to ensure they have the opportunity to participate in their interests. If the school does not offer a club to support your child's interests, talk with the teacher, the principal, and possibly other parents. Schools are always in need of afterschool clubs and volunteers to help engage students.

Again, make sure your child loves school. Put everything in place to make them successful.

Though some school activities cost, many activities are free. Additionally, if you are willing to be a club sponsor/volunteer, the school may be able to provide some resources for support. If you ask the right questions to the right person, anything is possible.

Expected answers:

"Gaming club."

"Basketball, football, other athletics."

"Chorus."

"Dancing."

Chapter 2: Act Like a Parent

Unacceptable answers:

"I am not interested in anything."

"I don't want to participate in afterschool activities."

"None of my friends have to join a club."

"Our school does not have any clubs."

What to do if you receive an unacceptable answer:

- Continue to encourage your child to seek interests in and beyond school. It is essential your child develop socially as well as academically.

- Try to balance encouragement with force. remember, just because you were a great <u>basketball</u> player does not mean your child will be interested in <u>basketball</u>. (Interchange the word "basketball" for your specific interest.)

- Listen to your child and let them pursue their interests (within reason). If you push too hard, they may push back!

Think Like a Teacher, Act Like a Parent

Question 19

What do you want to be when you grow up? How are you going to accomplish this?

Purpose of the question:
It is never too early to ask this question, and it is not possible to ask this question too many times. We are responsible for encouraging and exposing our children to different ideas. If you ask a three-year-old what they want to be when they grow up, you will hear everything from being a chef to being a super hero. As they grow older, their answers will change to the professions which they are most familiar. This concept is called *efficacy*. Simply stated, "If I can see it, I can be it." There is a good chance your child will want to be in either the same profession you are in or a profession celebrated in the community or on television (e.g., teacher, doctor, police officer, firefighter, etc.). These professions are noble, but there are so many more. Expose your child to many different professions. Introduce them to people working in those professions. Let them know the requirements and what they need to do in school.

Children (and some adults) do not understand the concept of delaying gratification. They see it. They want it. They do it. Many decisions are made without any regard for the future. Don't believe me? Just look at the tattoo explosion sweeping our youth. Someone needs to remind children there are certain things doctors, lawyers, policemen, firemen, teachers, and other desired professions do not do. I am not condemning tattoos or other forms of individual expression. I am simply suggesting that an 18 year old with a tattoo on their face and neck may be limiting their

Chapter 2: Act Like a Parent

marketability for future jobs, regardless of their mental abilities.

Simply, how you practice is how you play the game. If you practice looking like a thug, at some point you will become good at it. As a teacher, one of my favorite lines is, "Future doctors must behave like doctors," (change the word *doctor* as necessary). Saggy pants on a fifth grader does not lead to becoming a physician. Help your child create a plan for their future. How they dress is how they will be addressed! This may be unfair, sad, and maybe even stereotypical, but it's a reality in today's culture.

"I want to be a [model, football player, singer, etc.]" Many children are naturally going to lean toward professions they view as fun, easy, and glamorous. Remember, the law of efficacy states that people want to be what they see the most ("Monkey see, monkey do"). Your child's desire to have one of these professions may be related to what you allow them to be exposed to. Children do not need to watch or be exposed to adult television shows (including reality TV). Further, parents must take care not to live their life's dream through their child. Just because you wanted to "be like Mike" does not mean your child has the same aspiration. Vicarious living is never healthy, for either parent or child.

Children wanting glamorous professions need to see the preparation and sacrifice necessary to be famous. Wouldn't it be great for your son to spend one week working out with LeBron James, practicing golf with Phil Mickelson, working in the studio with the Steven Spielberg? Each of the aforementioned have dominated their respective profession and made it look easy, but each practiced their craft all day, every day.

83

Think Like a Teacher, Act Like a Parent

Pop Quiz:

Your eleven-year-old wants to be a detective. She has been talking about it for two years.

Which afterschool clubs may be a good fit?

_____

What elective courses should she take in junior high?

_____

What would be a good birthday gift for her?

_____

Who can you introduce her to in the community for a job shadow?

_____

Expected answers:

"I want to be a firefighter."

"I want to be a singer."

"I want to be a football player."

"I want to be a teacher."

Unacceptable answers:

"Nothing."

"I don't know."

Chapter 2: Act Like a Parent

7What to do if you receive an unacceptable answer:

- Teach your child that if they want to be a doctor, then they must emulate what doctors do.

- Exposure! Exposure! Exposure! Shape your child's reality. Take your child to work with you.

- Find local professionals willing to allow your child to shadow them for a few hours.

Think Like a Teacher, Act Like a Parent

Question 20

Who can you talk to if you have a problem (at school, at home, or anytime)?

Purpose of the question:
Children are humans. Like adults, children sometimes feel as though they are carrying the weight of the world on their shoulders. The major difference is that we, as adults, have been there before and understand "this too shall pass." Thus, we develop appropriate coping skills to assist us as the problem runs its course. If the problem does not move quickly enough, we seek out a loved one or a professional to discuss the problem with. Identifying and employing healthy coping strategies is essential for every human to have a productive life. Adults lacking healthy coping skills are apt to turn to drugs, crime, and other destructive behaviors.

What about our children? Even though their problems seem minor, they are major to the child trying to figure out this great big world. Pay attention to your child and try to figure out the following: How does your child cope with uncomfortable situations? Who taught him/her coping skills? Where is their "safe place?" Who can they run to for help? Trust me, they will run to someone for help. If it's not you, then who? The teacher? The coach? The neighborhood gang? An older cousin? A boyfriend?

86

Chapter 2: Act Like a Parent

Expected answers:

"When there is a problem I cannot solve by myself at school, I try to talk with my teacher first, then the school counselor, and then the principal. This is what the teacher told us to do."

"At home, I talk with you."

Unacceptable answers:

"I don't know."

"I don't talk with anyone. No one listens to me."

"I only talk to Ross, my best friend."

What to do if you receive an unacceptable answer:

- Ask the teacher to alert you of any problem your child takes to them. You have to know what is going on with your child, and it is critical that you approve of the school's approach to handling the conflict. Further, as children get older they can sometimes become a bit dramatic. If you think your child is spending too much time out of class with "problems," it is your responsibility to tell the school to call you before allowing your student to waste precious learning time in the counselor's office discussing the rumor of the day.

- Learn a variety of coping skills. Teach them and practice them with your child. Healthy coping is not just a skill set needed for school, but for the rest of life. Trouble and worry are a certainty. How we deal with our problems is essential to having a productive life.

87

Chapter 3:
School Discipline

FAQ's About School Discipline & the Law

Discipline Overview

The overall purpose of school discipline is to ensure a safe and secure learning environment. Perhaps the greatest disconnect between parent and school is in the area of student discipline. By its very nature, this area presents turmoil. Teachers teaching children seem like a natural function of the job. Teachers serving in place of the parents present a different set of concerns. The purpose of this section is to clear up a few misconceptions and inform you of the rights of parents, school personnel, and students. Much of this section is based on school law. We must note, however, that the law is fluid and always changing. This book does not stand as legal advice; its purpose is to give you an idea as to what is right and what is wrong. Should you have an issue with a school that you cannot resolve on your own, please seek legal advice from an attorney specializing in education.

To better understand student discipline, we must understand a few legal terms.

Due Process — Just as in the "real world," a student accused of an infraction must be given an opportunity to tell their side of the story. This can be written, spoken, typed, etc. Also, a student may decline to tell their side of the story. My suggestion is for a student to politely inform the administration that they will tell their side of the story

Think Like a Teacher, Act Like a Parent

once they have an opportunity to tell their parents what happened.

In Loco Parentis — This Latin term means "in place of the parent." Legally, teachers/schools are to act in place of the parents while the student is in their care. Schools are responsible for educating children and keeping them safe. Student discipline falls under this category.

Portal to Portal (Door to Door) — The school is responsible for a student from the time they leave their home to the time they return home. Yes, a student can be disciplined by the school for inappropriate behavior while walking to or home from school, even if the incident did not happen anywhere near the school.

Chapter 3: School Discipline

Frequently Asked Questions:

My child was kicked out of class. What should I do?

Children are children, and they will do things that are "childish." Sometimes children go overboard and the teacher may ask them to leave the classroom. When this is the case, a few steps should be taken by the teacher, by the parent, and by the student. The teacher's responsibility is to document the interventions used to handle the problem and to write a referral stating what happened during the incident. This incident write-up should be objective: Just the facts. If an act was not witnessed, then it should not be written. Also, the teacher must contact the parent to let them know *that* the student was removed, *why* the student was removed, and *how long* the student was removed from class. Finally, a school administrator must notify parents concerning any steps of recourse for the student to re-enter the classroom.

As a parent, your responsibility is to find out why your child was removed from class. Make sure your child knows what behavior you expect from them. Make sure the teacher knows that you have discussed the expected behavior with your child. And make sure the teacher is aware that you are an involved parent, and it is your expectation that your child be in class. Failing to talk to the teacher in this situation may result in your child being removed multiple times without you ever being notified. This can result in a loss of instructional time, suffering grades, and the lack of an opportunity to learn. By law, public schools are obligated to provide a free and appropriate education. Your child needs to be in class! If it is necessary for your child to be removed (and most of the time it is not necessary),

91

Think Like a Teacher, Act Like a Parent

then you need to be made aware as soon as possible. In this event, you need to go to the school (that same day) to find out exactly what happened.

The child's responsibilities are quite simple. The student knows the expectations of the classroom and the expectations of the school. They are to abide by these expectations. Make sure your child knows and understands that they should not escalate any situations. If the teacher asks them to remove themself from the classroom, your child should comply, go directly to the office, and contact you (the parent) from the school's phone.

Your child should not be placed in any alternative environment (that means a detention room or suspension room) without the school making many attempts to speak you first. Again, my advice to students is simply: do not talk until their parents are notified. Just like anywhere else, your child has the right to invoke the Fifth Amendment. They do not have to self-incriminate and can sit quietly until you respond. If this is the case, your child may be put in an alternative setting until the school hears from you. Again, your child does not have to talk. I suggest they politely say, "I want to talk to my parent before I give my statement to the school." Similar to any interrogation, they have the right to have counsel speak for them.

Chapter 3: School Discipline

My child was suspended. What should I do?

What is suspension? A suspension is when a student is removed from their normal learning environment. Many people believe suspensions are only out of school. That is not the case. Suspension can include both out of school and in-school. By law, if a student has been removed from the general learning environment then they are considered to be "suspended from school."

Students are suspended from school for major discipline infractions. Suspendable infractions are filed into two categories; Gross Misconduct and Gross Disobedience. In regards to suspension schools must be careful to have accurate details of the infraction. Students cannot be suspended for any subjective reasoning. Suspension should be the absolute last option when disciplining a student. As a parent, you have to know exactly why your child is being suspended.

When a student is to be suspended, the school has the responsibility of conducting a thorough and complete investigation. This investigation includes gathering the facts from witnesses. The suspended student will also be given the opportunity to tell their side of the story (due process). A student may, however, decline to give their side. I strongly urge parents to be available and/or present when their child is being questioned, or providing a statement.

Once the facts come out, and if indeed your child is to be suspended, the process will be as follows: You will receive a letter, a phone call, or some kind of contact from the school. Usually it is a letter saying that your child is being suspended for a certain period of time. The time period may be one day, three days, five days, or ten days. The

93

Think Like a Teacher, Act Like a Parent

maximum amount of time any student can be suspended is ten consecutive days. Anything beyond ten consecutive days is considered to be an expulsion with the possibility of being removed from school on a full-time basis. If your student is in a special education program, then the most they can be suspended is ten days per school year. Anything beyond ten days, the school must have an IEP meeting for your child (See Chapter 4: Special Education).

Upon returning to school, students should have an opportunity to make up any missing work. Be certain to get the schoolwork your child missed during the suspension. That work may be accepted at a discounted or a lessened grade. For example, if they receive 100% they may only receive 75% credit. Your child should be expected and have the option to make up any schoolwork they have missed.

Just because your child was out of school does not mean the education process stopped. After the suspension is complete, escort your child back to school that first day. Speak with the administrator. Ensure your child understands the rules and will follow them. Make sure you, the school, and your child all have the same understanding of the infraction, the punishment, and the future. Make sure your child understands their dismissal from school does not make them cool or a "rock star." This is not a time to be home playing Nintendo, Wii, or Xbox. Make sure your child understands the expectations and explain to them the seriousness of their offense. Hold your child accountable for their actions!

As a parent, you have the right to appeal the suspension, and the school must provide the appellate process in written format to you. My suggestion is that you appeal

94

Chapter 3: School Discipline

every suspension, even if your child is blatantly wrong. Again, the best place for your child is in school. At some point, suspension from school is not effective for either party. Children need to be in school. Therefore, it is imperative you appeal for every suspension to be shortened. Even if the suspension is not done away with totally, you want the shortest suspension time possible.

*To Review: If your child is suspended from school, you must take the following steps: Go to the school and talk with the administration to ensure you understand the reason for your child's dismissal. Appeal the suspension. Again, you want your child back in school as soon as possible, and many times the school will accommodate this request. Most importantly, make sure you explain to your child what they did wrong and hold them accountable. This is not the time to argue with the teacher or the school administration.

*If you truly feel your child was suspended from school for an unjust reason, take the following steps: (1) Contact the administrator that did the suspension. (2) Contact the school principal to see if you can appeal on that level. (3) Contact the school superintendent or the designee that hears the appeals. (4) Contact a school board member and discuss your opinion. After this is done, if you still have not gotten what you expect from the process, contact an attorney and be ready to talk about it. Many times, schools and school administrators are willing to negotiate to ensure the student gets back in school as soon as possible. Again, school administrators and teachers are not the enemy. They are usually friendly and interested in doing what is best for their students.

95

Think Like a Teacher, Act Like a Parent

Can my child be excluded from field trips?

Yes. If a student is misbehaving in school, why should the school be anxious to take that student on a trip? It is necessary for you to talk with your child about their behavior in school so they may participate in the fullness of the curriculum.

It is also essential that you avail yourself to chaperone field trips. I realize you have a job and a life away from your child's education. You must prioritize, and your child's education should be at the top of your list of priorities. If you are an involved parent, the school will bend over backwards to accommodate you and make sure your child gets the best education the school can offer.

Is it legal for school to search my child and their belongings?

Yes. It is legal for a school to search your child and their belongings. The Fourth Amendment of the U.S. Constitution protects all United States citizens against "unreasonable search." In the case of schools, administrators and law officials are allowed to search students if they have *probable cause* or *reasonable suspicion*.

Probable Cause — More than a bare suspicion but less than legal proof; grounds to suspect a person has committed a particular crime.

Reasonable Suspicion — Carefully considered assumption, based on specific facts, that a person is probably involved with criminal activity. A "reasonable" person would be able to assume the suspect is guilty.

Historically, when dealing with search and seizure, the

96

Chapter 3: School Discipline

court systems have been very lenient towards schools. The reason for this is schools are sensitive places which need to be kept safe. Therefore, the courts have taken the stance of better safe than sorry.

It must also be noted that items belonging to the school can be searched at any time, without reason. For example, lockers and desks belong to the school. Students are permitted to use them. At any point, a locker can be searched. The contents in the locker, belonging to a student, may or may not be searched depending on the establishment of probable cause or reasonable suspicion. To be quite honest, school personnel can conduct a search at any time. In many instances, the nature of children, especially older children, supports reasonable suspicion.

As mentioned in the prior section, when being questioned/interrogated for the purpose of a school investigation, your child does not have to speak. Again, note that they may be detained or presumed guilty for not speaking. However, I do recommend a parent or advocate be present when a student is being questioned. This recommendation is not to "buck the system." Multiple adults in authoritative positions can intimidate children. No matter the incident, a child is still a child and needs an advocate. Further, keep in mind that school rules do not trump the Constitution of the United States. If a student is being detained and a police officer is present, the officer must provide students with the Miranda Rights ("You have the right to remain silent, etc."). In many states, the questioning and interrogation must stop if the students requests to speak with an attorney. However, police can continue interrogating if a student asks to speak with their parent, mentor, pastor, etc.

97

Think Like a Teacher, Act Like a Parent

Can a school take away my child's cell phone or other electronic devices?

Yes! Anything that is seen to be a disruption to the learning environment can be taken away or confiscated. The school does have the right to take such items away. However, the items must be returned within a reasonable timeframe. Just because a child breaks the school rule by bringing such an item to school does not make the item the school's property. The child or parent still owns the cell phone or electronic device; the school is just holding it for a short period of time. To define a reasonable timeframe, different standards have been used. In most schools, a reasonable timeframe is one day for the first offense and one week for the second offense. Anything beyond that calls for a parent to come pick up the item.

Though schools do have the right to confiscate items such as cell phones, schools do not have the right to go through the call log on the cell phone without reasonable suspicion or probable cause. Therefore, students who have their phones confiscated still fall under the protection of the Fourth Amendment to the U.S. Constitution (search and seizure). Just because an item is taken away does not give the school the right to go through the call log or the text messages.

As cell phones and handheld electronic devices grow in popularity, schools are becoming more and more stringent about such policies. Most schools have a permission slip or some kind of active document that parents and students must sign pertaining to cell phones and other handheld devices.

98

Chapter 3: School Discipline

Why are such policies necessary? Well just imagine a typical junior high conversation: He said – that she said – that her cousin said – you were going to beat me up. I called my cousin, put it on Facebook, tweeted it, sent out a text message, and recorded a video with my cell phone. Now a small junior high school rumor turns into a major, press-worthy event. Or what if, jokingly or maliciously, a student takes their cell phone into the locker room and makes a video of your child changing clothes?

Schools must act in the best interest of hundreds of students at once. I realize your child would never do anything to break a rule. However, someone else's child may not be as perfect as yours! ☺

Chapter 4:
Special Education (In Plain English)

Special Education Overview

By title alone, Special Education may be one of the more difficult areas to understand about public education. Not only is it difficult to understand, but special education is filled with laws. Therefore the rules of the federal government outweigh the rules of schools. Special Education and the IDEA Special-Education ACT of 1975 insist that students with special needs receive the same learning opportunities as their "general education" peers. Furthermore, students with special needs must be afforded equal opportunity and equal access to the entire education program. Special Education should only serve as a bridge between a student disability and the general education curriculum. For example, a student who has trouble processing information should be a part of the regular classroom. However, special education adaptations and interventions should be put in place to assist this student as much as possible.

There are many forms of special education and varying disabilities classified into special education. Such disabilities include learning, behavioral, as well as physical limitations. Schools and teachers have many resources to assist students with any kind of disability. A disability does not mean the student needs to be in courses that restrict, or limit the offered curriculum. In fact, special-education law insists each student be in the Least Restrictive Environment (LRE).

Think Like a Teacher, Act Like a Parent

With that said, just because Ray Charles could not see did not mean he could not learn to read. What should we do to assist Ray Charles? We teach him how to read using braille. His immediate physical disability does not mean he is not a genius in his own right. He simply needed a few accommodations to enrich the curricular possibilities. Even students with special needs have a genius within them, and it's up to the school, teachers, and parents to assist that genius in coming out. To level the playing field for students with special needs, schools have very specific plans and interventions that must be documented and put into place for students. There are two plans schools use to address special needs: "504 Plans" and "IEP's"

Chapter 4: Special Education (In Plain English)

IEP vs. 5-0-4 Plan

"IEP" **Individualized Education Program:**	"5-0-4" **Section 504 of the Rehabilitation Act of 1973:**
Student program or curriculum that is different, altered, or accommodated when compared to the general education curriculum	Assists in providing students with disabilities access to equal educational opportunities; the general curriculum remains the same, however extended access is granted
Special/Altered instruction including "Modifications" to actual curriculum materials as needed	"Accommodations" for accessing standard program or curriculum materials (i.e. extended time to take test)
Used for specified disabilities including Behavioral/Emotional, Specified Learning Disabilities, Hearing, Vision, etc.	Much less specific – available to students with physical or mental disability that limits one major life activity
Individuals with Disabilities Education Act (IDEA) – Education Law	Americans with Disabilities Act (ADA) – Civil Rights Law
Disability must be listed; progress, short-term goals, modifications, behavioral/ social/emotional skills plan may be necessary, summer services, transport needs, placement recommendation	Clear objectives, care and self-care details, resource access, health/medical monitoring, emergency plan, classroom/testing subtleties must be considered, communication and notification instructions
A student covered under IDEA on an IEP is automatically covered under ADA's Section 504	A student covered under ADA's Section 504 is not necessarily covered by education law under IDEA
Progress reporting	No progress reporting

103

Think Like a Teacher, Act Like a Parent

Special Education Questions and Answers

Special-education is just what it says: Special. The laws of special education are created by the federal government, and as such, special education is not necessarily a function of the school district. Federal laws always trump the laws or rules of school districts. For this reason, this section is written from a legal perspective rather than a school-rule perspective.

Further, I am not an attorney. This section is filled with recommendations and information. This section is not legal advice. If you find yourself in a situation that requires legal advice specific to schools or special-education, please contact an attorney dealing specifically within the areas of schools and special education.

Rather than give you questions to ask the special education provider, I find it necessary to inform you of your rights and provide information about special education in plain English to help you gain an understanding of all the legalese involved.

What is special education?

Special education is a free and appropriate public education provided to students with special identified needs and or disabilities. This can include physical handicaps, learning disabilities, and gifted education.

Most people are familiar with special education as it relates to handicap and learning disabled students. However, it is important to remember gifted education is considered a form of special education.

Chapter 4: Special Education (In Plain English)

When considering special education, it is of utmost importance to acknowledge that all students are general education students first and foremost.

Do schools have to be totally handicapped accessible?

No. Schools do not have to be totally handicapped accessible. Doing so could cost millions of dollars and that burden would have to be paid by the taxpayers. Schools do not have to be 100% handicap accessible, but all programs must be handicap accessible. Every program offered in the school and every class offered at the school must be offered in areas which every student can easily get to. For example, if a school does not have an elevator and Honors Physics is only located on the third floor, it may be necessary to move this class, to allow a student with a physical disability to take this class.

What is mainstreaming?

Mainstreaming is the term used for ensuring all students, especially special education students, have an equal opportunity to the least restrictive learning environment. To be more specific, students with special needs are only held out of the general population of students when absolutely necessary to meet the needs of their disability.

For this reason, it is common to see special needs students in class with the general population of students. It is not uncommon for the special needs student to have an assigned teacher assistant with them. Other times the regular teacher will be able to differentiate the curriculum enough to ensure the special education student's needs are met.

Think Like a Teacher, Act Like a Parent

What is a self-contained classroom?

A self-contained classroom is a classroom in which the special-education students are not permitted to interact with the general population of students. Plainly, the student will only be in classes with other students of similar disability. This is mostly done with students that have extreme mental impairment, or extreme behavioral issues.

Who recommends testing?

Recommendations for testing for special education can be made by various people. Parents, teachers, school personnel, and even community agencies familiar with the student's needs are able to recommend students for testing. Just because the student is recommended for special education testing does not mean the student will receive special education services.

I frequently remind parents they have the final decision as to what happens with their child. You have the responsibility of gathering sufficient information when making any decisions. So just because someone else thinks your child needs (or does not need) special education, does not mean you should go along with their decision. Make an informed and well thought out decision on the matter.

What is an Individualized Education Program (IEP)?

An Individualized Education Program (IEP) is a written plan specific to the needs of the student and the disability. An IEP trumps the academic policies of the school and the educational program a traditional student must take to meet graduation requirements. For this reason, it is essential for an IEP be crafted with the utmost care. IEPs are developed by teams which include general education teachers, special education teachers, school counselors, school social workers, school psychologists, school

106

Chapter 4: Special Education (In Plain English)

administration, parents, children, and any other professional pertinent to ensuring the student's needs are being met. Again IEP's are legal documents and trump the traditional school curriculum.

What does an IEP look like?
IEP's must include the following:
1. Statement of the student's present status and current academic performance

2. Measurable academic and behavioral goals

3. Services that will be provided for the student, including personnel and any assistive technologies

4. An explanation and account given for times the student will not be with the general population of students

5. Statement of accommodations and interventions deemed necessary to assist in the student academic achievement or behavioral goals

6. Date in which interventions will begin and date for reevaluation of all goals and interventions

*Notice the sample IEP at the end of this section.

What if I disagree with the findings?
You have the responsibility to do what you believe is best for your child. You do not have to accept the results of any special needs testing or evaluation of your child. Testing provided by the school is free of charge and completed by school officials. However, if you choose to have your child evaluated by an independent party (personal psychologist,

Think Like a Teacher, Act Like a Parent

family physician, etc.) then the cost is to be paid by you. Additionally, if the school finds your child is in need of special education services and you disagree, you are not obligated to have your student participate in special education. Plainly, if you do not want your student to have an "IEP" and receive support services from the school, then the school will not provide any additional support for your child.

*I sincerely hope you and your child's school have a very trusting and productive relationship. If the school recommends special education services, you and the school should be able to work together to create a plan that will maximize your child's potential.

What are "labels?"
To better determine the necessary accommodations for a student, titles and labels are applied to their specific disability. There are many special education labels, and these are constantly evolving. A few of the standard labels given are:

LD - Learning Disabled
BD - Behavior Disordered
OHI - Other Health Impairments
ADHD - Attention Deficit Hyperactivity Disorder
HI - Hearing Impaired
ED - Emotionally Disturbed
TBI - Traumatic Brain Injury

Will my child be "labeled?"
If your student qualifies for special education services, they should be treated like any other student in the school. Sadly, there are times when students with special needs are referred to by their disability. "Labeling" is not right, but truthfully... it does happen.

108

Chapter 4: Special Education (In Plain English)

My child is very active (possibly AD/HD). Does he/she belong in special education?

Probably not. Try a few of the interventions listed at the end of this section and talk with the teacher about learning styles and differentiated instruction.

*I am personally not a fan of medication and believe that should be the last resort. Give your child a chance to self-correct life before adding medication into the mix. Ultimately, medications can be mood altering, addictive and have serious side effects.

If identified, how long is my child eligible to receive special education protections?

A student may remain in special education until they are age 21, or until they have made satisfactory progress throughout the evaluation/re-evaluation period, which may serve to substantiate that the student no longer needs the accommodations, support, and interventions associated with special education.

What is the timeframe between re-evaluations?

The parent or the school can request an IEP team meeting at any time. During this meeting, you can discuss progress and changes to the individual education plan. School-based re-evaluations are generally conducted every two or three years or as deemed necessary by the IEP case manager. .

As a parent, do I have any financial obligations to the IEP or special education of my child?

Not necessarily. Everything written in the IEP is to be provided for the student free of charge. Provisions will be made by the school district to ensure the student has everything necessary to be successful. This may include assistive technologies, special assistants, interpreters, or

109

Think Like a Teacher, Act Like a Parent

additional tutors. However, other supports identified by the parents but not written in the IEP, if purchased, are purchased by the parent without reimbursement from the school.

What are easy interventions?

Prior to any special education evaluations, there are a few things you can do as a parent to intervene with your child's lack of achievement in a traditional classroom setting.

- Search for outside academic support/tutoring services.
- Make sure your child is getting proper rest. (8-10 hours of sleep per night.)
- Encourage a healthy/balanced diet. (Donuts and a juice box is not a meal!)
- Provide a structured home environment (Homework time, bed time, etc.)
- Have your child practice 20 minutes of Reading and Math every night.
- Stay home! (Children need some down time. They cannot always be on-the-go!)
- Choose relevant social interactions (Girl Scouts, YMCA, church, youth sports, etc.)
- Give your child a hug and kiss every night!

Chapter 4: Special Education (In Plain English)

Sample IEP

Attached is a sample IEP. Though all IEPs are not formatted the same, the important information included are: the diagnosed disability, goals, measurements, accommodations, and supports. IEP's are legally binding documents and should be taken very serious. Schools, parents, and outside agencies must work closely to create an educational program that best benefits the student. Do not agree to anything you are not comfortable with. If uncertain, consult with a local educational advocate.

Think Like a Teacher, Act Like a Parent

INDIVIDUALIZED EDUCATION PROGRAM
Verdana Elementary School

IEP Team Meeting Date: October 7, 20XX

IEP Implementation Date (Projected Date when Services and Programs Will Begin): October 15, 20XX

Student Name: _____Bill Smith_____

DOB: _____Sept. 18, 20XX_____

Grade: _4_   **Anticipated Year of Graduation:** _20XX_

School District: _Verdana School District_

Parent Name: _Mr. & Mrs. Smith_

Address: _678 9th Street_

Phone: _(H) 555-555-555_

Disability: ___Learning Disabled (Reading)___

Chapter 4: Special Education (In Plain English)

IEP TEAM/SIGNATURES*

The Individualized Education Program (IEP) Team makes the decisions about the student's program and placement. The student's parent(s), the student's regular teacher and a representative from the local education agency are required members of this team. A regular education teacher must also be included if the student participates, or may be participating in regular education. Signature on this IEP documents attendance, not agreement.

_____

Parent   Special Education Teacher

_____

LEA   School Psychologist

PROCEDURAL SAFEGUARDS NOTICE

I have received a copy of the Procedural Safeguards Notice. The District has informed me whom I may contact if I need more information.

Parent signature: _____

Received: _____

Think Like a Teacher, Act Like a Parent

Individualized Education Program

I. SPECIAL CONSIDERATIONS THE IEP TEAM MUST CONSIDER BEFORE CREATING THE IEP. ANY FACTORS CHECKED MUST BE ADDRESSED IN THE IEP.

Is the Student Blind or Visually Impaired?

_X_ No

____ Yes - Team must provide for instruction in Braille and the use of Braille unless the IEP Team determines, after an evaluation of the child's reading and writing skills, needs and appropriate reading and writing media (including an evaluation of the child's future needs for instruction in Braille or the use of Braille), that instruction in Braille or the use of Braille is not appropriate.

Is the Student Deaf or Hearing Impaired?

_X_ No

____ Yes - Team must consider the child's language and communication needs, opportunities for direct communications with peers and professional personnel in the child's language and communication mode, academic level, and full range of needs, including opportunities for direct instruction in the child's language and communication mode in the development of the IEP.

_X_ COMMUNICATION NEEDS

____ ASSISTIVE TECHNOLOGY, Devices and /or Services

Chapter 4: Special Education (In Plain English)

____ LIMITED ENGLISH PROFICENCY

____ BEHAVIORS THAT IMPEDE HIS/HER LEARNING or that of OTHERS

____ TRANSITION SERVICES

____ OTHER (Specify) _____

STUDENT'S PRESENT LEVELS OF EDUCATIONAL PERFORMANCE:

Based on the Woodcock-Johnson Educational Testing, Bill performs at a K-Grade 2 achievement level in reading. These results show significant differences from his expected performance based on his cognitive ability.

Bill's reading level for decoding and fluency are at a Grade 2 level. During classroom instruction involving reading, he relies on initial sounds along with picture and context clues to guess at unknown words. Bill knows 42 sight words on the first grade list. When reading, Bill shows difficulty discriminating between similar and dissimilar sounds.

Bill is successful in following directions when instructions are broken down and modeled. His 3rd grade teacher reports that when she uses this approach with Bill, he is more successful.

Think Like a Teacher, Act Like a Parent

HOW THE STUDENT'S DISABILITY AFFECTS INVOLVEMENT AND PROGRESS IN GENERAL EDUCATION CURRICULUM (Include the child's strengths and needs, which will affect the student's involvement and progress in the general curriculum.):

Based on Bill's educational levels, he has difficulties in the areas of Reading and Writing. In contrast, Bill is progressing with his peers in the area of Science, Mathematics, and social studies (especially when passages are read to him).

Bill has many friends and is well liked by adults and his peers. Adaptations that appear to impact on Bill's success in the classroom are: direct instruction, multisensory techniques during reading, word banks, and directions broken down into single units with modeling and visual clues.

Student's strengths:

- Identify words that begin with the same sound
- Articulation skills
- Rapidly name all letters of alphabet
- Computational and problem solving levels are at third grade level

Chapter 4: Special Education (In Plain English)

Student's needs:

- Regulated, intense, and direct instruction in reading using structured language and multisensory techniques in order to develop phonological, decoding, and automaticity skills.

- Directions and instructions broken down into single units with modeling and visual clues.

Think Like a Teacher, Act Like a Parent

II. GOALS AND OBJECTIVES:

MEASURABLE ANNUAL GOAL 1: Bill will demonstrate phonological awareness skills by blending and segmenting syllables in 2 - 4 syllable words and individual phonemes in 3 - 4 phoneme words with 90% accuracy.

SHORT TERM OBJECTIVE/BENCHMARK	EXPECTED LEVEL OF ACHIEVEMENT	METHOD OF EVALUATION
Bill will identify (by clapping) the number of syllables in 2 - 4 syllable words presented orally.	90% accuracy	Weekly oral review
Bill will identify the initial and final sounds in 3 - 4 phoneme words presented orally.	80% accuracy	Weekly oral review
Bill will blend and segment 2 - 3 syllable words presented orally.	90% accuracy	Weekly oral review
Bill will blend and segment 3 phoneme words presented orally.	90% accuracy	Weekly oral review

REPORT OF PROGRESS ON ANNUAL GOALS

How goals will be measured: Weekly oral reviews using the established sequential list of sounds mastered.

How progress will be reported: Use of written (narrative) quarterly report sent home to parent at the end of each marking period with progress charts.

Chapter 4: Special Education (In Plain English)

MEASURABLE ANNUAL GOAL 2: Bill will read text at the second grade level at 100 wpm with 90% accuracy.

SHORT TERM OBJECTIVE/BENCHMARK	EXPECTED LEVEL OF ACHIEVEMENT	METHOD OF EVALUATION
Bill will orally say the beginning and ending sounds when presented with words	100% accuracy	Teacher review using sequential list of sounds taught
Bill will orally identify the beginning blends when presented with words	90% accuracy	Teacher review using sequential list of blends taught
Bill will correctly read all "cvc" (consonant-vowel-consonant) words	90% accuracy	Teacher review using Cs & Vs that have been taught
Bill will correctly read all "cvcv" (consonant-vowel-consonant- vowel) words	80% accuracy	Teacher review using words containing Cs & Vs that have been taught

REPORT OF PROGRESS ON ANNUAL GOALS

How goals will be measured: Weekly reading review taken from the second grade materials in use completed by resource room teacher.

Think Like a Teacher, Act Like a Parent

How progress will be reported: Monthly phone conference between teacher and parent — the dates of which are recorded on the following grid. Each phone conference will discuss the teacher probes from the previous two weeks.

MEASURABLE ANNUAL GOAL 3: Bill will improve comprehension of language (semantic knowledge) of receptive vocabulary, categorization, and classification skills with 90% accuracy in targeted language probes.

SHORT TERM OBJECTIVE/BENCHMARK	EXPECTED LEVEL OF ACHIEVEMENT	METHOD OF EVALUATION
Bill will demonstrate comprehension of 3 curriculum-based adjectives and 3 adverbs in 4/5 targeted language selections/activities.	80%	Bi-monthly targeted language probes
Bill will categorize and classify 5 language concepts by property, location and function in 4/5 targeted language activities.	80%	Bi-monthly targeted language reviews
Bill will demonstrate understanding of 10 multiple-meaning words in 9/10 targeted language activities.	90%	Bi-monthly targeted language reviews
Bill will recall 5 factual details using visual imagery from 9/10 oral presentations given by the teacher.	90%	Selected oral presentations

Chapter 4: Special Education (In Plain English)

REPORT OF PROGRESS ON ANNUAL GOALS

How goals will be measured:
Informal assessment/curriculum based assessments with authentic curricular probes.

How progress will be reported: report card

First Marking Period

After testing Bill's identification of the number of syllables in a word using weekly oral probes, the resource room teacher reports that Bill has mastered, with 90% accuracy or better, these concepts and can readily indicate the correct number through clapping. If he continues to make this amount of progress, Bill will complete this goal by the end of the school year.

Second Marking Period

Bill maintains the skills that he mastered the first marking period. He is able to identify initial and final phonemes with 70% accuracy when presented with 2 - 3 phoneme words orally. Bill is able to blend and segment 2 - 3 syllable words with 80% accuracy, as well as 3 phoneme words with 70% accuracy.

Third Marking Period

Fourth Marking Period

Think Like a Teacher, Act Like a Parent

III. SPECIAL EDUCATION/RELATED SERVICES:

A. PROGRAM MODIFICATIONS AND SPECIALLY DESIGNED INSTRUCTION: *(Specially designed instruction may be listed with each goal/objectives.)*

1. A systematic structured language reading program using direct instruction, decodable texts, and multisensory techniques including visual imagery strategies.

2. Word lists derived from his reading lessons that can be used for speaking exercises.

3. Age appropriate phonological activities Computer-Assisted Instruction for phonics reinforcement.

4. Self-monitoring checklist

5. Use of nonverbal, physical, and visual cues to prompt teacher assistance

6. Adapted science and social studies materials (study guides, modified direction, emphasis on responses that are verbal and demonstration).

B. SUPPORTS FOR THE CHILD PROVIDED FOR SCHOOL PERSONNEL:

None

C. EXTENDED SCHOOL YEAR:

N/A

Chapter 4: Special Education (In Plain English)

D. PARTICIPATION IN STATE AND DISTRICT-WIDE ASSESSMENTS

STUDENT PARTICIPATION – STATE ASSESSMENTS

_X_ Student will participate in the ISAT with accommodations.

STUDENT PARTICIPATION – DISTRICT ASSESSMENTS

_X_ Student will participate in the District assessments with accommodations.

Think Like a Teacher, Act Like a Parent

IV. LEAST RESTRICTIVE ENVIRONMENT (LRE)

EDUCATIONAL PLACEMENT

Resource Room Learning Support

Explanation of the extent, if any, the student **will not participate** with non-disabled children in the regular class and in the general education curriculum:

Bill will participate in all aspects of the general education program in the regular classroom except during the time that reading is being taught. He will receive daily reading instruction in the Resource Room for 30 minutes. However, he will be included in all other portions of language arts. He will receive speech and language support twice a week (30 minutes per session) during a portion of the day that will not interfere with academic instruction.

Percentage of time the student receives special education outside of the regular education classroom:

_X_ Less than 21% outside of the regular education classroom

____ 21-60% outside of the regular education classroom

____ 61% or more outside of the regular education classroom Location of Program: Universal Elementary

Chapter 4: Special Education (In Plain English)

V. TRANSITION PLANNING

1. Will the student be 14 years of age or older during the term of this IEP?

____ No - (Not necessary to complete this Section)

_X_ Yes - Team must address the student's courses of study and how the course of study applies to components of the IEP.

2. Will the student be 16 years of age or older during the term of this IEP or is the student younger and in need of transition services as determined by the IEP Team?

____ No - (Not necessary to complete this Section)

_X_ Yes - Team must address and complete this Section

* Again, this is only a sample. Each IEP differs based upon the individual needs of the student. The purpose of this sample is to familiarize you with what the document may include.

Chapter 5:
A Short Conclusion

To summarize, there are a few things you should remember:

1. Children are more important than cars, jobs, homes, etc.

2. Your child is your responsibility.

3. Schools are great places filled with great teachers and staff members that love children.

4. Schools have their own language. If you do not speak this language, your child may suffer.

5. Get involved with your child's school.

6. Children are children and prone to make a few mistakes. Knowing how to advocate for them, especially when they make mistakes, is essential.

7. No one should know your child better than you.

8. Children want, desire, and need attention. We are all busy, but if you don't give your child attention someone else will. (That isn't always a good thing.)

9. Schools offer specials services. All services offered to children must be relevant and rigorous. If you believe your child is not being challenged, take action immediately.

10. Encourage your child to "ride the road of education to its natural end."

About the Author

Dr. James Carter Harden III is on a mission to use the power of education to increase life opportunities for children. James has accomplished this mission as a teacher, a principal, a professor, and as an educational consultant. James' commitment and passion for educating children has yielded him numerous honors and accolades in the field of education.

James holds a Bachelor's degree in Social Sciences, a Master's in Education Leadership, and a Doctorate (PhD) in Education and Organizational Leadership.

James is the extremely happy husband of Lashonna Nicole Harden and the loving father of Shaun Carter and Nina Olivia Harden. Together with his wife and the *We Teach Parents* community (www.weteachparents.com), James is on a mission to genuinely increase life opportunities for all children!

About the Author

Dr. James Carter Hardon III is on a mission to use the power of education to increase life opportunities for children. James has accomplished this mission as a teacher, a principal, a professor, and as an educational consultant. James' commitment and passion for educating children has yielded him numerous honors and accolades in the field of education.